N. T. Wright

EVIL
AND THE
JUSTICE
OF
GOD

IVP Books

An imprint of InterVarsity Press
Downers Grove, Illinois

InterVarsity Press
P.O. Box 1400, Downers Grove, IL 60515-1426
Internet: www.ivpress.com
E-mail: email@ivpress.com

Published in the United States of America by InterVarsity Press, Downers Grove, Illinois, with permission from
Society for the Promotion of Christian Knowledge.

InterVarsity Press® is the book-publishing division of InterVarsity Christian Fellowship/USA®, a movement of
students and faculty active on campus at hundreds of universities, colleges and schools of nursing in the United
States of America, and a member movement of the International Fellowship of Evangelical Students. For
information about local and regional activities, write Public Relations Dept., InterVarsity Christian Fellowship/
USA, 6400 Schroeder Rd., P.O. Box 7895, Madison, WI 53707-7895, or visit the IVCF website at
<www.intervarsity.org>.

Unless otherwise indicated, Scripture quotations are the author's translation.

Cover design: Cindy Kiple
Cover image: istockphoto.com

ISBN 978-0-8308-3415-0

Printed in the United States of America ∞

 InterVarsity Press is committed to protecting the environment and to the responsible use of
natural resources. As a member of the Green Press Initiative we use recycled paper whenever
possible. To learn more about the Green Press Initiative, visit <www.greenpressinitiative.org>.

Library of Congress Cataloging-in-Publication Data

Wright, N. T. (Nicholas Thomas)
  Evil and the justice of God / N. T. Wright
    p. cm.
  Includes bibliographical references and indexes.
  ISBN-13: 978-0-8308-3398-6 (cloth: alk. paper)
  ISBN-10: 0-8308-3398-6 (cloth: alk. paper)
  1. Good and evil. 2. Christianity and justice. 3.
Redemption—Christianity. I. Title.
  BJ1401.W72 2006
  231'.8—dc22
                                        2006020864

P	18	17	16	15	14	13	12	11	10	9	8	7	6	5	4
Y	28	27	26	25	24	23	22	21	20	19	18	17	16	15	

In memory of those who died

in New York and Washington on September 11, 2001,

around the Indian Ocean in December 2004,

in New Orleans and the Gulf Coast in August 2005,

and in Pakistan and Kashmir in October 2005

CONTENTS

PREFACE

After working for some years on a major book on the resurrection, I resolved at the start of 2003 that I would turn my attention to the meaning of Jesus' crucifixion. But as soon as I began to think how I might approach the subject, I realized that there was something else I had to do first. When Christians talk about what Jesus accomplished in his death, they usually say something about his cross as the answer to, or the result of, evil. But what is evil?

The same question presented itself to me for a very different reason. Between September 11, 2001, when terrorists flew airplanes into the Twin Towers in New York and into the Pentagon in Washington, and my reflecting on the cross and the problem of evil in early 2003, the topic of "evil" had suddenly become hot. American President George W. Bush had declared that there was an "axis of evil" which had to be dealt with. British Prime Minister Tony Blair announced that the task of the politician was to rid the world of evil. Commentators on the left and on the right expressed doubts about both the analysis and the solution—doubts which the war in Iraq and its aftermath have amply justified.

I turned my reflections into five lectures which I delivered at Westminster Abbey, where I was then working, in the first half of 2003. I then attempted to summarize my thesis in a television program made by Blakeway Productions and first screened on Channel 4 in the U.K. on Easter Day 2005; copies of this film are available from Blakeway (www.blakeway.co.uk). I am very grateful to David Wilson, the producer, and to Denys Blakeway himself, for understanding what I was trying to say and enabling me to communicate it in a very different medium. Those who saw the program and were puzzled by what I did not manage to say in the 49 minutes available to me may perhaps be mollified by the fuller version offered in the present book.

Having said that, I do not pretend for a moment that I have here provided a full or even a balanced treatment either of the problem of evil or, more especially, of the meaning of Jesus' crucifixion. The central chapter of this book approaches Jesus' death from one angle which I believe to be deeply fruitful, but I am well aware that a more complete account of the meaning and saving effect of Jesus' death would need to raise and answer far more questions than I have even mentioned, and to deal with biblical passages and theological and philosophical ideas for which there is no space here. I hope, however, that this will at least point in the direction of further work.

In the first lecture—now the first chapter—I used as one of my controlling images the biblical picture of the wild, untamed sea. I was then all the more horrified when, on December 26, 2004, a tsunami ripped across the Indian Ocean, smashing people and communities to pieces. Then, like the rest of the world, I had an awful sense of déjà vu when Hurricane Katrina drowned New Orleans and a large section of the American Gulf Coast in August 2005. When I asked myself to whom the present book should be dedicated, I could think of no better answer than to honor the memory of those who died in those two disasters and the subsequent earthquake in Pakistan and Kashmir, along with the victims of September 11, 2001. They are a reminder that "the problem of evil" is not something we will "solve" in the present world, and that our primary task is not so much to give answers to impossible philosophical questions as to bring signs of God's new world to birth on the basis of Jesus' death and in the power of his Spirit, even in the midst of "the present evil age."

N. T. Wright
Easter 2006

Evil Is Still a Four-Letter Word

The New Problem of Evil

In the new heaven and new earth, according to Revelation 21, there will be no more sea. Many people feel disappointed by this. Looking at the sea, sailing on it and swimming in it are perennial delights, at least for those who don't have to make a living by negotiating its treacherous habits and untimely bad moods. As a regular sea watcher and occasional swimmer, I share this sense of surprise and disappointment. But within a larger biblical worldview we can begin to make sense of it.

The sea is of course part of the original creation. Indeed, it appears earlier in Genesis 1 than the dry land, and both the land and then the animals come out of it. It is part of the world which God says, at the end of the six days, is "very good." But already by Genesis 6, with the story of Noah, the rising waters of the flood pose a threat to the entire world that God has made, from which Noah and his floating zoo are rescued by the warnings of God's grace. From within the good creation itself, it seems, come forces of chaos harnessed to enact God's judgment.

We then hear no more of the sea until we find Moses and the Israelites standing in front of it, chased by the Egyptians and at their wits' end. God makes a way through the sea to rescue his people and once more to judge the pagan world; it is the same story, in a way, though now in a new mode. And as later Israelite poets look back on this decisive, formative moment in the story of God's people, they celebrate it in terms of the old Canaanite creation myths: YHWH (the biblical name of the God of Israel) is King over the flood (Ps 29:10); when the floods lift up their voices, YHWH on high is mightier than they are (Ps 93:3-4); the waters saw YHWH and were afraid, and they went backwards (Ps 77:16; 114:3, 5). Thus, when the psalmist describes his despair in terms of being up to his neck in deep waters, as in Psalm 69, this is held within a context where YHWH is already known as the one who rules the raging of the sea and even makes it praise him (Ps 69:1, 34).

But then we find in the vision of Daniel 7, a passage of enormous influence on early Christianity, that the monsters who make war on the saints of the Most High come up out of the sea. The sea has become the dark, fearsome place from which evil emerges, threatening God's people like a giant tidal wave threatening those who live near the coast. For the people of ancient Israel, who were not for the most part seafarers, the sea came to represent evil and chaos, the dark power that might do to God's people what the flood had done to the whole world, unless God rescued them as he rescued Noah.

It may be (though this might take us too far off our track) that one of the reasons we love the sea is because, like watching a horror movie, we can observe its enormous power and relentless energy from a safe distance. Alternately, if we go sailing or swimming on it, we can use its energy without being engulfed by it. I suspect there are plenty of Ph.D. theses already written on what's going on psychologically when we do this, and I haven't read them. We would, of course, find our delight turning quickly to horror if, as we stood watching the waves, a tsunami were suddenly to come crashing down on us, just as our thrill at watching a gangster movie in the theater would turn to screaming panic if a couple of heavily armed thugs came out of the screen and threatened us personally. The sea and the movie, seen from a safe distance, can be a way of saying to ourselves that, yes, evil may well exist—there may be chaos out there somewhere—but at least, thank goodness, we are all right, we are not immediately threatened by it. And perhaps this is also saying that, yes, evil may well exist inside ourselves as well—there may be forces of evil and chaos deep inside us of which we are at best only subliminally aware—but they are under control: the sea wall will hold, the cops will get the gangsters in the end.

Of course in the movies of the last decade or two, things may not work out so well, which may tell us something about how we now perceive evil both in the world and in ourselves. That perception, and the Christian attempt to understand it, to critique it and to address it, is the subject of this book. I began by wanting to write something about the meaning of Jesus' crucifixion; having written at length about Jesus' resurrection, it seemed the appropriate balancing subject. But the more I thought about that, the more I realized that in order to speak meaningfully about the cross one must say at least something about evil, the problem which, in classic theology, the cross has decisively addressed.

But as soon as I thought of speaking about evil, I realized that this is a timely, not to say urgent, topic. Everybody is talking about evil. As I said in the preface, after September 11, 2001, President Bush and British Prime Minister Tony Blair both spoke of "evil" as the attack's main cause and declared their intention of dealing with it. British Prime Minister Tony Blair declared ambitiously that we should aim at nothing short of ridding the world of evil. The day I drafted this chapter, I glanced sleepily at a newspaper being read in the seat in front of me in an airplane and saw an enormous headline inviting us to look at "the evil faces" of two members of the so-called Real Irish Republican Army. The public and press cried "Evil!" at the terrible murder of two little girls in the English town of Soham in 2003, and we say the same about the sudden rise of gun crime in the streets of our cities or the violence which followed the devastation of New Orleans by Hurricane Katrina in August 2005.

The odd thing about this new concentration on evil is that it seems to have taken many people, not least politicians and the media, by surprise. Of course they would say that there has always been evil, but it seems to have come home to the Western world in a new way. The older discussions of evil tended to be abstract, with so-called natural evil (represented by the tidal wave) and so-called moral evil (represented by the gangsters). Just as Auschwitz posed the problem in a new way for the previous generation (at least for those who allowed themselves to reflect on it), September 11, 2001, and the "natural" disasters of the tsunami in the Indian Ocean and the hurricane on the American Gulf Coast, have now jumpstarted a fresh wave of discussion about what evil is, where it comes from, how to understand it and what it does to your worldview, whether you're a Christian or an atheist or anything else. And, not least, what if anything can be done about it.

From the Christian point of view, there will be in that sense no more sea in the new heavens and new earth. We are committed, within the worldview generated by the gospel of Jesus, to affirming that evil will finally be conquered, will be done away with. But understanding why it's still there as it is, and how God has dealt with it and will deal with it, how the cross of Jesus has anything to do with that, how it affects us here and now, and what we can do here and now to be part of God's victory over evil—all these are deep and dark mysteries which the sudden flurry of new interest in evil opens up as questions, and to which many of us, myself included, have not been used to giving much attention, let alone to offering answers.

I put it like this because (if you see what I mean) I am not an expert on evil. There are those who do engage in that dubious specialization. I have learned from them already and I hope to do so in the future. I am, to this extent, standing in the noble tradition of continuing my theological education in public. I am in implicit dialogue at various points with some recent writing on the subject, though I make no pretense to have mastered the field. What I want to do can be seen in three stages, each of which subdivides into a further three.

First, I will try to lay out the problem as it appears in our contemporary culture (chapter one) and to place beside it the classic statements of God's saving justice in the Jewish and Christian traditions, focused particularly on the cross of Jesus Christ (chapters two and three). Then I will propose a way of speaking Christianly and creatively about the problem of evil and about what, under God, Christians are supposed to be doing about it (chapter four). At that point I shall raise three areas of great contemporary interest in each of which the problem of evil, if not articulated and addressed, will cause terrible difficulties and dangers: the questions of global empire, of criminal justice and punishment, and of war. In the final chapter I shall continue to examine these by considering the corporate as well as the deeply personal meaning of forgiveness.

In this initial chapter, then, I shall try to describe some ways in which the problem of evil presents itself today in a new form; or, to put it another way, I shall argue that politicians and media have tried to live as though evil weren't so much of a problem after all, and that they are having to wake up to the fact that *evil* is still a four-letter word. I will then suggest that the new ways in which the problem of evil has been articulated within postmodernity—and postmodernity is, importantly, precisely a restatement of the problem—are deficient in certain important respects. I then want to propose that if we are to see more clearly what is going on, we need to factor certain things into our understanding which are normally screened out. Finally, I shall suggest ways in which this question impinges on Christian thinking.

THE NEW PROBLEM OF EVIL

So to my first and longest section: the new problem of evil. Why "new"?

The older ways of talking about evil tended to pose the puzzle as a metaphysical or theological conundrum. If there is a god, and if he is (as classic Jewish, Muslim and Christian theology all claim) a good, wise and supremely powerful god, then why is there such a thing as evil? Even if you're an atheist, you face the problem the other way around: is this world a sick joke, which contains some things that make us think it's a wonderful place and other things which make us think it's an awful place, or what? You could of course refer to this as the problem of good rather than the problem of evil: if the world is the chance assembly of accidental phenomena, why is there so much that we want to praise and celebrate? Why is there beauty, love and laughter?

The problem of evil in its present metaphysical form has been around for at least two-and-a-half centuries. The earthquake that shattered Lisbon on All Saints' Day 1755 shattered as well the easy optimism represented by the previous generation. Think of Joseph Addison's great hymn, "The Spacious Firmament on High," with its repeated affirmation that all who look at the sky, the sun, the moon, the stars and the planets are bound to realize that they are the good workmanship of a good creator:

> In reason's ear they all rejoice,
> And utter forth a glorious voice,
> For ever singing as they shine,
> "The hand that made us is divine."

We may venture to doubt whether Addison could have written that after 1755 or, if he had, whether anyone would have been quite so willing to sing it. We who have heard of so many further disasters, both natural and man-made, can only perhaps continue to sing it either because we have learned a hard-won natural theology in the teeth of the negative counterevidence or because we have not stopped to think. But my point is that from 1755 on, as Susan Neiman has shown recently in her brilliant book *Evil in Modern Thought*, the history of European philosophy can best be told as the history of people trying to come to terms with evil. Lisbon precipitated the now standard distinction between natural evil (the tidal wave, the earthquake, the hurricane) and moral evil (the gangsters, the terrorists), and that has remained a feature; but the wrestlings of the great enlightenment thinkers like Voltaire and Rousseau, and the massive schemes of Kant and Hegel themselves, can be understood as ways of coping with evil. And when we come further forward to Marx and Nietzsche and to the twentieth-century thinkers (not least Jewish thinkers) who have wrestled with the question of meaning following the Holocaust, we find a continuous thread of philosophical attempts to say what has to be said about the world as a whole and about evil within it.

Unfortunately (in my view) the line of thought which has emerged from this, and which has characterized the popular understanding of the Western world as a whole, and of Britain and the United States perhaps in particular, is very unsatisfactory. I refer to the doctrine of progress, as expounded loftily by Hegel and as we find, in watered-down forms, as a constant in much contemporary thinking. Hegel suggested, more or less, that the world was progressing by means of the dialectical process: first (A), then its opposite (B), then a synthesis of the two (C) and so on. Everything was moving toward a better, fuller, more perfect end; and if there had to be suffering on the way, if there had to be problems as the dialectic unwound, so be it; such things are the broken eggs from which delicious omelets are being made.

This belief in automatic progress, which we find at the same time in poets such as Keats, was in the air in the pantheism of the Romantic movement and in the philosophy of Malthus which was so influential in generating and sustaining the Western belief that Europe and North America were on the leading edge of human development, and that this justified the imperial economic expansion which was such a feature of the nineteenth century. This belief, already well established in the prevailing culture, was given an enormous boost by the popularization of Charles Darwin's research and its application to fields considerably more diverse than the study of birds and mammals on the Galapagos Islands. The heady combination of technological achievement, medical advances, Romantic pantheism, Hegelian progressive Idealism and social Darwinism created a climate of thought in which, to this day, a great many people—not least in public life—have lived and moved. In this climate, the fact that we live "in this day and age" means that certain things are now to be expected; we envision a steady march toward freedom and justice, conceived often in terms of the slow but sure triumph of Western-style liberal democracy and soft versions of socialism. Not to put too fine a point on it, when people say that certain things are unacceptable "now that we're living in the twenty-first century," they are appealing to an assumed doctrine of progress—and of progress, what's more, in a particular direction. We are taught, often by the tone of voice of the media and the politicians rather than by explicit argument, to bow down before this progress. It is unstoppable. Who wants to be left behind, to be behind the times, to be yesterday's people? The colloquial phrase "That's *so* last-year" has become the ultimate putdown: "progress" (by which we often simply mean a variation in fashion) has become the single most important measuring rod in society and culture.

This belief in progress has received at least three quite different challenges, and it is remarkable that it has survived them all and still flourishes. For many, the First World War destroyed the old liberal idealism. When Karl Barth wrote his first commentary on Romans in 1919, his main message was that it was time to listen for the fresh word of God coming to us from outside instead of relying on the steady advance of the kingdom of God from within the historical process. Fyodor Dostoyevsky, in *The Brothers Kara-*

mazov, has a haunting passage in which he considers the possibility that the world might advance toward perfection at the cost of torturing a single innocent child to death, and he concludes that the price is already too high. Auschwitz destroyed, one would have thought forever, the idea that European civilization at least was a place where nobility, virtue and humanizing reason could flourish and abound. The deep roots of the Holocaust in several strands of European thought—not least Hegel himself, who regarded Judaism as a manifestation of the wrong sort of religion—have to be unraveled and deconstructed.

Thus, as I said, it seems remarkable that the belief in progress still survives and triumphs. The nineteenth century thought it had gotten rid of original sin; of course, it had to find replacements, and Marx and Freud offered some, producing explanatory systems and offering solutions to match: new doctrines of redemption which mirror and parody the Christian one. And somehow, despite the horrific battles of Mons and the Somme during World War I, despite Auschwitz and Buchenwald, despite Dostoyevsky and Barth, people still continue to this day to suppose that the world is basically a good place and that its problems are more or less soluble by technology, education, "development" in the sense of "Westernization," and the application, to more and more regions, of Western democracy—and, according to taste, of either Western social-democratic ideals or Western capitalism, or indeed a mixture of both.

This state of affairs has led to three things in particular which I see as characterizing the new problem of evil. First, we ignore evil when it doesn't hit us in the face. Second, we are surprised by evil when it does. Third, we react in immature and dangerous ways as a result. Let me unpack each of these in turn.

First, we ignore evil except when it hits us in the face. Some philosophers and psychologists have tried to make out that evil is simply the shadow side of good; that it's part of the necessary balance in the world, and that we must avoid too much dualism, too much polarization between good and evil. That, of course, leads straight to Nietzsche's philosophy of power and by that route back to Hitler and Auschwitz. When you pass beyond good and evil, you pass into the realm where might is right, and where anything that reminds you of the old moral values—for instance, a large Jewish community—stands in your way and must be obliterated.

But we don't need to look back sixty years to see this. Western politicians knew perfectly well that Al-Qaeda was a force to be reckoned with; but nobody really wanted to take it too seriously until it was too late. We all know that chronic national debt in many of the poorer countries of the globe is a massive sore on the conscience of the world, but our politicians—even the sympathetic ones—don't really want to take it too seriously because from our point of view the world is ticking on more or less all right, and we don't want to rock the economic boat. We want to trade, to build up our economies. "Choice" is an absolute good for everyone; therefore if we offer both Coca-Cola and Pepsi to starving, AIDS-ridden Africa, exploiting a huge untapped market while adding tooth decay to its other chronic problems, we are furthering its well-being. We all know that sexual licentiousness creates massive unhappiness in families and individual lives, but we live in the twenty-first century, don't we, and we don't want to say that adultery is wrong. (We should perhaps note that only two generations ago many communities regarded adultery the way they now regard pedophilia, which is worrying on both counts.)

I grew up at a time when censorship was being dismantled right, left and center. Censorship, we were told, was the only real obscenity. Whatever people wanted to do or say was basically good; we should celebrate whatever instincts we found inside ourselves; people shouldn't be allowed to control what other people did. Indeed to this day the word *control* is spoken with a sneer, as in the phrase "control freak," as though the basic moral norm was for there to be no control—just as the basic slogan of large McWorld-type companies is that there should be "no boundaries." We live in a world where politicians, media pundits, economists and even, alas, some late-blooming liberal theologians speak as if humankind is basically all right, the world is basically all right, and there's nothing we should make a fuss about.

So then, second, we are surprised by evil when it hits us in the face. We think of small towns as pleasant, safe places and are shocked to the core when two little girls are murdered by someone they obviously knew and trusted. We have no categories to cope with that; but neither do we have categories to cope with the larger renewed evils, with renewed tribalism and genocide in Africa or the renewed "Balkanization" of the Balkans themselves. We like to fool ourselves that the world is basically all right, now that so many countries are either democratic or moving that way and now that globalization has in theory enabled us to do so much, to profit so much, to know so much. Then we are puzzled as well as shocked by the human tidal wave that crashes on our shore, the seemingly endless tragic wall of humanity that comes to Western countries seeking asylum, bringing with it several (though not, we may suppose, more than a small fraction) who are looking not for safety from persecution or tyranny but rather for the secrecy necessary to further their terrorist intentions.

Indeed terrorism itself takes us by surprise, since we have become used to imagining that all serious questions should be settled in a round-table discussion, and we are puzzled that some people still think that doesn't work, and that they need to use more drastic methods of getting their point across. And ultimately we are shocked again and again by the fact of death. That which our forebears took for granted (having large families because a sudden epidemic could carry off half of them in a few days) is banished from our minds, except in horror stories. Similarly, death is banished from our societies, as fewer and fewer people die in their own homes and beds. And it is banished, too, from our deep-seated societal imagination, as the relentless quest for sexual pleasure—and sex, of course, is a way of laughing in the face of death—occupies so much energy and enthusiasm, and dulls the aching reminders that come flooding back with every funeral we see, every murder the television brings into our living rooms. We ignore evil when it doesn't hit us in the face, and so we are shocked and puzzled when it does.

Third, as a result, we react in immature and dangerous ways.

Having decreed that almost all sexual activity is good and right and commendable, we are all the more shrill about the one remaining taboo, pedophilia. It is as though all the moral indignation which ought to be spread more evenly and thoughtfully across many other spheres of activity has all been funneled on to this one crime. Child abuse is of course stomach-turningly disgusting, but I believe we should beware of the unthinking moralism which is so eager to condemn it simply because we hate the thought of it rather than on properly thought-out grounds. "Morality" like that can be, and often is, manipulated. Lashing out at something you simply know by intuition is wrong may be better than tolerating it. But it is hardly the way to build a stable moral society.

One of the most obvious and worrying instances of this phenomenon was the reaction to the events of September 11, 2001, in the United States (and to a degree in the United Kingdom as well). That appalling day rightly provoked horror and anger. But the official response was exactly the kind of knee-jerk, unthinking, immature lashing out which gets us nowhere. Let me not be misunderstood. Thousands of innocent victims met, of course, a tragic, horrible and totally undeserved death. The terrorist actions of Al-Qaeda were and are unmitigatedly evil. But the astonishing naivety which decreed that the United States as a whole was a pure, innocent victim, so that the world could be neatly divided up into evil people (particularly Arabs) and good people (particularly Americans and Israelis), and that the latter had a responsibility now to punish the former, is a large-scale example of what I'm talking about—just as it is immature and naive to suggest the mirror image of this view, namely that the Western world is guilty in all respects, and that all protesters and terrorists are therefore completely justified in what they do. In the same way, to suggest that all who possess guns should be locked up or that everyone should carry guns so that good people can shoot bad ones before they get to their tricks is simply a failure to think deeply about what's going on. The second-stage horror of the flooding of New Orleans—the violence of those with nothing to lose and the eager buying up of guns by those who wanted to protect themselves and their property—should, but may not, teach us a lesson.

Lashing out at those you perceive to be "evil" in the hope of dealing with the problem—say, dropping copious bombs on Iraq or Afghanistan because of September 11—is in fact the practical counterpart of those philosophical theories that purport to "solve" the problem of evil. Various writers have suggested, for instance, that God allows evil because it creates the special conditions in which virtue can flourish. But the thought that God decided to permit Auschwitz because some heroes would emerge is hardly a solution to the problem. In the same way, the thousands of innocent civilians who died in Iraq and Afghanistan bear mute testimony to the fact that often such "solutions" simply make the problem worse—and I don't just mean because they harden and indeed generate opposition. Just as you cannot eliminate evil by act of Congress or by a philosophical argument, so you cannot do so with high explosives.

The immature reactions to evil can perhaps be seen close up if we ask ourselves how we react to evil in our own lives or immediate circumstances. What are you angry about right now? Who has done something which you feel is unjust or unfair? How do you cope with it? How do you come to terms with it? We react so often in one of two ways. We can project evil out on to others, generating a culture of blame: it's always everyone else's fault, it's society's fault, it's the government's fault, and I am an innocent victim. Claiming the status of victim has become the new multicultural sport, as people scramble for the moral high ground in which they can emerge as pure and clean, and everybody else is to blame.

Alternatively, we can project evil onto ourselves and imagine we are to blame for it all. This is one of the normal causes of depression; but the issue is wider than just psychological states. Politically we oscillate between those who tell us that all the ills we face are the fault of someone else—terrorists, asylum-seekers, drug dealers, criminals—and those who tell us, in the classic pop psychology of the 1960s and 1970s, that we are all guilty, that the terrorists are terrorists because of what we've allowed to happen in their countries, that the asylum seekers are fleeing the effects of our previous foreign policies, that the drug dealers deal in drugs because we've destroyed their other indigenous livelihoods, and that the criminals are the victims of the affluent society. The fact that there is more than a grain of truth in both caricatured sides of this equation doesn't help. The culture of blaming everyone else (resulting in lawsuits, victim exaltation and self-righteousness) and the culture of blaming oneself (resulting in depression and moral and social paralysis) are likewise immature and inadequate responses to the problem of evil as it presents itself, not so much in our metaphysical discussions as on our streets and television screens. This is the current new problem of evil. We have discovered that *evil* is still, after all, a four-letter word; but we don't have a clue what to do with it or about it. And, let me add, ignoring it isn't an answer either.

I shall discuss a little later the question of how we begin to grow up in our reaction to evil: how we take account of it in every dimension and arrive at a more mature worldview which will allow us to address it more satisfactorily. But I now want to turn to look at the attempt to address evil, indeed in a sense to base a worldview on it, that we know as "postmodernity."

THE NEW NIHILISM: POSTMODERNITY

I have spoken and written elsewhere about the postmodern turn in literature, culture and theology, and there is no space here to develop this in any depth. Suffice it to say that there have been many movements in contemporary European and American culture since World War II in which all claims to truth, all claims to power and all claims to disinterested action or thought are deemed to be motivated in fact by selfish desires into which they can be translated or "deconstructed." "It's all about money," said Marx; "It's all about sex," said Freud; "It's all about power," said Nietzsche; and, though much of Europe scoffed at them for the first half of the twentieth century, the second half saw them come into their own in areas as diverse as literary criticism, architecture and sociology. Truth is under attack on all sides, even as we insist more and more on truthfulness in terms of record keeping and checking up on one another. As Bernard Williams showed in his book *Truth and Truthfulness*, this self-contradictory state of affairs—increased demands for truth and increased difficulty in discerning it—is the result of a slow-growing but now all-pervasive culture of suspicion.

Though postmodernity has roots in thinkers from a century or more ago, the particular way in which it has arisen and the particular form it has taken has a lot to do with the horror of the Holocaust. The philosopher Theodor Adorno declared that one cannot write poetry after Auschwitz, and it may be that, at one level at least, the postmodern theorists were saying that one cannot tell the truth either. If mainstream European culture could produce the Holocaust, surely we should suspect everything else as well. But postmodernity doesn't stop there. The problem of evil which it highlights so remorselessly goes deeper than simply suggesting that all human claims are flawed; it deconstructs humans themselves. There is no longer an "I": just a swirling mass of emotions, of signifiers, of impulses, meaning that "I" am in a constant state of flux. The moral imperative left over from low-grade existentialism (that one should be true to one's deepest self) collides with the postmodern claim that one's deepest self is a fluid, unstable thing: Jazz bassist Charles Mingus says of himself in his autobiography, "I am three. . . . There's all kinds of emotion to play in music, but the one I'm trying to play is very difficult. It's the truth of what I am. It's not difficult to play the mechanics of it, but it's difficult because I'm changing all the time."

This, too, I think, is a kind of response to the problem of evil.

Postmodernism, in recognizing that we are all deeply flawed, avoids any return to a classic doctrine of original sin by claiming that humans have no fixed "identity" and hence no fixed responsibility. You can't escape evil within postmodernity, but you can't find anybody to take the blame either. We should not be surprised that one of the socio-cultural phenomena which characterize postmodernity is that of major disasters for which nobody takes the blame, such as when a horrific train crash is traced to faults in the line which were well-known and not repaired months in advance but for which no single company executive, nor even a board, can be held responsible. Postmodernity encourages a cynical approach: nothing will get better and there's nothing you can do about it. Hardly surprisingly, this has produced a steady rise in the suicide rate, not least among young people who (one might have thought) had so much to look forward to, but who had imbibed postmodernity through every pore. Not that this is new. Epictetus, that hard-bitten first-century philosopher, would have understood, even though he would have scoffed at the intellectual posturing underneath it all.

After this it may come as a surprise to learn that in all sorts of ways I believe postmodernity is to be welcomed. It offers an analysis of evil which the mainstream culture I described earlier still resists; it deconstructs, in particular, the dangerous ideology of "progress." As I have argued elsewhere, I regard the main function of postmodernity under God to be the preaching of the doctrine of the Fall (the truth of a deep and fatal flaw within human nature) to the modernist, post-eighteenth-century arrogance that supposes it has solved the world's problems. But in addition to the cynicism I just mentioned, there are two particular problems with the postmodern analysis of evil which should drive us to look further and deeper.

First, postmodern analysis is essentially, for the reasons already given, dehumanizing. There is no moral dignity left because there is nobody left to bear the blame. To shoulder responsibility is the last virtue left open to those who have forsworn all other kinds. To have even that disallowed is to reduce human beings to mere ciphers. Most of us, not least the genuine victims of crime and abuse, find that both counter-intuitive and disgusting. Human beings are (within reason and within certain limits) responsible agents and must continue to be regarded as such. Here I find most moving the testimony of George Steiner, who at the end of his intellectual autobiography, *Errata*, declares that though he cannot believe for sure in God, he can be quite sure that there is such a thing as evil and that human beings must take their fair share of responsibility for it. That is a plea for a gloomy but authentic humanism at the end of an inhuman century.

Second, the analysis of evil offered by postmodernity allows for no redemption. There is no way out, no chance of repentance and restoration, no way back to the solid ground of truth from the quicksands of deconstruction. Postmodernity may be correct to say that evil is real, powerful and important, but it gives us no real clue as to what we should do about it. It is therefore vital that we look elsewhere, and broaden the categories of the problem from the shallow modernist puzzles on the one hand and the nihilistic deconstructive analyses on the other. This brings us to the third section of this chapter.

TOWARD A NUANCED VIEW OF EVIL

When we look for larger, broader, more sustainable analyses of evil, we find of course that the major worldviews have all had ways of addressing it. The Buddhist says that the present world is an illusion and that the aim of human life is to escape it. This has several affinities with classic Platonism, though Plato was concerned as well that actual justice and virtue should work their way out into the world of space, time and matter, even though reality lay elsewhere. The Hindu says that evils that afflict people (and indeed animals) in the present life are to be explained in terms of wrongs committed in a previous life and expiated through an obedient following of one's karma in the present—a worldview which attains a deeply satisfying solution at one level at the cost of enormous and counterintuitive problems at other levels.

The Marxist, selectively elaborating some aspects of Hegel's thought, says that the world is moving in a determined way toward the dictatorship of the proletariat, and the problems on the way, not least the absolute need for violent revolution, are the growing pains which will be justified by the final result. The glorious end will validate the messy means; when you taste the omelet, you will understand why the eggs needed breaking. The Muslim, if I have understood Islam correctly, says that the world is in a state of wickedness because the message of Allah through Muhammad has not yet spread to all people; the solution is for Islam to be brought to the world, generating a sharp distinction between the great majority of Muslims who see this as a peaceful process and the small minority who want to achieve it through *jihad*.

What might a Christian view of evil, or for that matter a Jewish view, look like? How would it differ from any of the above? That is of course the subject of this book, and I defer even the start of an answer to later. But some notes may be appropriate to help us think about what should be included within a serious analysis of evil. There are three elements which need to be factored into our thinking at this point.

The first element is to recognize the flaw in assuming that the Western type of democracy is perfect, complete, the climax of a long process of wise and noble libertarianism stretching back to Magna Carta. Basically this contemporary assumption—a sort of low-grade version of that way of telling modern history which implies that things always automatically proceed in a liberalizing direction—has all kinds of problems, not least that present democratic institutions are themselves in a state of crisis. In the United States, we see a politics of the super-rich and a seemingly unstoppable belief in the right of the United States to rule the world, whether by economic or military means. In my own country of Great Britain, we have an increasingly presidential style of government, a marginalized parliament and a disaffected electorate. In Europe, we have multiple ironies and tensions, corruptions and deceits, which are neither addressed nor solved by phrasing the debates in terms of a simplistic mudslinging match between Europhiles and Europhobes.

Are we really so sure that Western-style government is the only or even the best type? For myself, I still agree with Churchill that democracy is the worst possible form of government, except for all those other forms that are tried from time to time. I certainly do not want to live under any other system. But I find myself increasingly wondering whether, to some extent at least, it is right to expect, say, Afghanistan or Iraq to adopt a version of it. What I am pleading for is a recognition that simply waving a flag called "Western democracy" doesn't actually solve the problem of evil as it presents itself in our corporate and social environment.

The second element which must be factored in is the psychological one. The famous American psychotherapist M. Scott Peck was for many years an agnostic. He learned his psychiatry according to the standard model in which there was no such thing as evil. But at around the same time as, to his own surprise, he came into the Christian faith, he came to recognize that in some cases at least it was not enough to regard certain patients, or in some cases the families of certain patients, as simply ill or muddled or misguided. He was forced to come to terms with a larger, darker power, for which the only word was *evil*. He wrote his book *People of the Lie* to articulate this unpopular viewpoint.

Of course, it has been recognized at least since Aristotle that there is such a thing as weakness of will, *akrasia* in Aristotle's terminology. We all know what it is to intend to do something good and to do something bad instead. What psychiatry, according to Peck, ought to confront is the fact that it is possible for humans to be taken over by evil, to believe a lie and then to live by it, to forget that it is a lie and to make it the foundation of one's being. Whether the difference between ordinary weakness of will and being taken over by a lie so totally that you fully believe it is a difference of degree or quality I cannot say, though I suspect it is the latter. What I think we must come to terms with is that when we talk about evil we must recognize, as neither modernity nor postmodernity seems to me to do, that there is such a thing as human evil and that it takes various forms. These forms include the state in which the people concerned are absolutely convinced, and will often argue very persuasively, that they are not only in the right but are the ones who are leading the way.

In *People of the Lie* Peck argues, against all his traditional liberal education and previous understanding, that there is such a thing as a force or forces of evil which are supra-personal, supra-human, which appear to take over humans as individuals or, in some cases, as entire societies. Using the language of the demonic is so fraught with problems and so routinely sneered at within liberal modernism that it might seem dangerous even to mention it. Yet many of the most serious analysts of the last century have been forced to use this language as a way of getting at, and trying to account for, what happened. The most memorable in my mind is Thomas Mann, in his great and harrowing novel *Doctor Faustus*. His Faust-character, it gradually emerges, is an image of Germany itself, selling its soul to the devil and finding itself taken over by a power greater than its own, a terrible power which would destroy many others but finally would destroy itself.

We have only begun, I think, to work seriously at understanding this element, this dimension, in the problem of evil. Neither modernism nor postmodernism cares for it, and many Christian theologians, aware of the dangers of an unhealthy interest in the demonic, steer well clear of it, as indeed I myself have done in most of my work. But as Walter Wink has argued strongly in his major work on the powers, there is a great deal to be said for the view that all corporate institutions have a kind of corporate soul, an identity which is greater than the sum of its parts, which can actually tell the parts what to do and how to do it. This leads to the view that in some cases at least, some of these corporate institutions—whether they be industrial companies, governments or even (God help us) churches—can become so corrupted with evil that the language of "possession" at a corporate level becomes the only way to explain the phenomena before us.

This leads to the third point, which was made movingly by Aleksandr Solzhenitsyn when he returned to his native Russia after long years of exile. He greeted all the people he met on his journey across Russia, including those local bureaucrats who had tyrannized their fellow citizens under the Communist system but who had stayed on in office after 1989. Some objected: what was Solzhenitsyn doing fraternizing with these people who had been part of the evil system? No, he responded, the line between good and evil is never simply between "us" and "them." The line between good and evil runs through each one of us. There is such a thing as wickedness, and we must distinguish between small and low-grade versions of it and large and terrible versions of it. We must not make the trivial mistake of supposing that a one-off petty thief and a Hitler are exactly alike, that the same level of evil is attained by someone who cheats in an exam and by a Bin Laden. But nor must we suppose that the problem of evil can be either addressed or solved if we trivialize it in the other way, of labeling some people "good" and other people "bad."

These three elements—a willingness to concede that we may not have got democracy right, and that it may not be the universal panacea for all ills; a recognition of a depth-dimension to evil, a supra-personal element within it; and the acknowledgement that the line between good and evil runs through us all—are necessary, I suggest, if we are to make any headway with our understanding of evil, whether at a metaphysical, theological, political or personal level. I hope to be able to factor them into the discussion in subsequent chapters. What I want now to do in concluding the present chapter is to say something briefly about the task ahead, not least from the Christian point of view.

CONCLUSION

The big question of our time, I have argued, can be understood in terms of how we address and live with the fact of evil in our world. Growing out of the traditional philosophers' and theologians' puzzlement, the problem of evil as we face it today on our streets and in our world won't wait for clever metaphysicians to solve it. What are we going to *do*? If we are not to react in an immature way, either by ignoring evil, or by declaring it's all the other person's fault, or by taking the blame on ourselves, we need a deeper and more nuanced way of answering the question many (not least the politicians) are asking: Why is this happening? What, if anything, has God done about it? And what can we or should we be doing about it?

The Christian belief, growing out of its Jewish roots, is that the God who made the world remains passionately and compassionately involved with it. Classical Judaism and classical Christianity never held an immature or shallow view of evil, and it is one of the puzzles of the last few centuries how mainstream philosophers from Leibniz to Nietzsche could think and write about the problem of evil as though the Christian view could be marginalized or dismissed with cheap caricature. Were there no theologians to stand up and take issue? Did the case simply go by default?

In particular, there is a noble Christian tradition which takes evil so seriously that it warns against the temptation to "solve" it in any obvious way. If you offer an analysis of evil which leaves us saying, "Well, that's all right then; we now see how it happens and what to do about it," you have belittled the problem. I once heard a leading philosophical theologian trying to do that with Auschwitz, and it was squirmingly embarrassing. We cannot and must not soften the blow; we cannot and must not pretend that evil isn't that bad after all. That is the way back to cheap modernism. As I said earlier, that is the intellectual counterpart to the immature political reaction of thinking that a few well placed bombs can eliminate "evil" from the world. No: for the Christian, the problem is how to understand and celebrate the goodness and God-givenness of creation and, at the same time, understand and face up to the reality and seriousness of evil. It is easy to "solve" the problem by watering down one side or the other, saying either that the world isn't really God's good creation or that evil isn't really that bad after all. What I have argued in this chapter is that the problem isn't simply a matter of what we think of as philosophy or theology; the failure to address the question lies at the root of our puzzlement about several complex and urgent problems in the immediate political and social spheres.

The questions that ought to be occupying us as a society, never mind as a church, are these: How can we integrate the various insights about evil which the greatest thinkers and social commentators have offered? How can we offer a Christian critique of them where necessary? And how can we tell the Christian story in such a way that, without attempting to "solve" the problem in a simplistic way, we can nevertheless address it in a mature fashion, and in the middle of it come to a deeper and wiser faith in the creator and redeemer God whose all-conquering love will one day make a new creation in which the dark and threatening sea of chaos will be no more?

Noah's flood, after all, was a sign that even God the Creator was sorry that he had made the world. But, not least through the sign of the rainbow, it becomes the means of a new start—a new covenant. If we can work toward understanding and being the willing agents of both the divine tears over the world's evil and the fresh creativity that sends out the dove to find new olive branches emerging from the waters of chaos, we shall, I think, be on the right track. The sea is powerful, but God the Creator is more powerful still. *Evil* may still be a four-letter word. But so, thank God, is *love*.

2

What Can God Do About Evil?

Unjust World, Just God?

In the first chapter I offered a large-scale overview of the problem of evil and suggested some markers that need to be put down as we try to think soberly and Christianly about it. Evil, I argued, isn't just a philosophical problem but a practical one. By trying to ignore or belittle it, the Enlightenment tradition stands convicted of culpable arrogance, while the critique of the Enlightenment offered in postmodernity—important though it is—can't offer any fresh solutions. I concluded by suggesting that Western democracy itself isn't to be thought of as an automatic solution to the problem of global evil, and that we need to take seriously both the supra-human powers of evil and the fact that the line between good and evil runs not between "us" and "them" but through every individual and every society.

I deliberately didn't begin to look at the Bible—apart from the initial imagery about the sea—principally because I wanted to take a preliminary walk around the problem as it presents itself in today's world before asking what resources there are within the Jewish and Christian traditions for approaching it. Now I shall make up for this by diving straight into the biblical material and seeing what it has to offer. It will, however, be obvious that I cannot say everything that could be said in a single chapter on the Old Testament and a single one on the New Testament. All we can do is to scratch the surface; but sometimes even scratches can provide vital clues.

The title of this chapter reflects my perception of one highly important feature of the Old Testament. What our Western philosophical tradition inclines us to expect—and indeed to ask for— is an answer to the question, What can God *say* about evil? We want an *explanation*. We want to know what evil really is, why it's there in the first place (or at least in the second place), why it's been allowed to continue, and how long this will go on. These questions are in the Bible, but frustratingly they don't receive very full answers, and certainly not the sort of answers that later philosophical traditions would consider adequate.

The Psalms regularly ask how long this wretched state of affairs will go on (e.g., Psalms 13:1; 79:5). There are dark hints about wickedness being allowed to go on for a while so that, when God judges, that judgment will be seen to be just (e.g., Genesis 15:16; Daniel 8:23). There are fleeting glimpses of the place of evil as an intruder into God's good creation (Genesis 3; 6), though this is never set out to our full satisfaction. The Old Testament oscillates among three things: evil seen as idolatry and consequent dehumanization; evil as what wicked people do, not least what they do to the righteous; and evil as the work of the "satan" (a Hebrew word meaning "accuser").

None of these are exactly explanations. The Bible simply doesn't appear to want to say what God can say about evil. That provides a powerful extra argument for the point I made in the last chapter, that at least one tradition within Christian thought has warned against our trying to explain it at all.

The Old Testament talks quite a lot about what God can do, is doing and will do about evil. It may be possible that we can work back from there to some account of what the Bible thinks evil is, and why it's there, but that's seldom if ever the primary focus. Insofar as the Old Testament offers a theodicy (an explanation of the justice of God in the face of counterevidence), it's couched not in the terms of later philosophy but in the narrative of God and the world, and particularly the story of God and Israel.

In fact—and this is crucial, I think, for understanding the Old Testament as a whole—what the Bible gives us is both much less and much more than a set of dogmas and ethics, much less and much more than a "progressive revelation," a steady unfolding of who God is. The Old Testament isn't written in order simply to "tell us about God" in the abstract. It isn't designed primarily to provide information, to satisfy the inquiring mind. It's written *to tell the story of what God has done, is doing and will do about evil*. (This is true of most of the individual books as well as the canonically

shaped Old Testament as we have it, both in the Hebrew order of
books and in the English one.) This happens at several different
levels, and I shall explore them presently; but we must grasp from
the outset that the underlying narrative logic of the whole Old Testament assumes that this is what it's about.

Let me map three levels in particular so we can see where we
shall be going. First, the entire Old Testament as we have it hangs
like an enormous door on a small hinge, namely the call of Abraham in Genesis 12. This, it appears, is intended by God the Creator to address the problem evident in Genesis 3 (human rebellion
and the expulsion from the Garden of Eden), Genesis 6—7 (human wickedness and the flood) and Genesis 11 (human arrogance, the tower of Babel and the confusion of languages).

Within that story we discover a second-order problem: Israel,
the children of Abraham, may be the carriers of the promise, but
they turn out to be part of the problem themselves. This unwinds
through a massive and epic narrative, from the patriarchs to the
exodus, from Moses to David, through the twists and turns of the
Israelite monarchy, ending finally with Israel in exile.

Within *that* story we discover a third level of the problem: it is
not only the human race that has rebelled, not only Israel that has
failed in its task, but as individuals humans in general find themselves to be sinful, idolatrous and hard-hearted.

The result of this is clear on page after page of the Old Testament. True, "the problem of evil" often appears in the Old Testament in the familiar form of wicked pagan nations oppressing
God's poor and defenseless people. But again and again the histor-

ical and prophetic writings remind Israel that the problem goes deeper than "us" and "them." The problem of the individual, which in much Western thought has been made central to philosophical and theological understanding, is presented in the Bible as a subset of the larger problem of Israel, of humankind and of creation itself. If we learn to read the Old Testament in this way (which we often don't when we work through it in small segments, whether in church or in private) we shall begin, I think, to glimpse the whole forest as well as the particular and sometimes puzzling trees.

TO RENEW THE BLESSING

We do well to begin at the beginning. In the first main section of this chapter, I shall expound the way in which Genesis 12, and the narrative that flows from it, addresses the triple question of evil as it is presented in Genesis 1—11. In the second section I shall engage with the multiple problems that arise when the family of Abraham is itself discovered to be riddled with evil. The third section will draw the focus more tightly into the period of the Babylonian exile and look at three biblical passages, including the book of Job, which wrestle with the question more deeply and poignantly than anywhere else. This will lead to some conclusions about the way in which the Old Testament leaves us facing the problem of evil, with powerful themes expounded but not concluded.

We start with God's decision to call Abraham (or Abram as he still was; for ease I shall use the longer form throughout) and to promise that through him and his family, all the families of the earth would be blessed (Genesis 12:1-3). This promise is repeated over and over in various forms to Abraham and then to Isaac and Jacob. It isn't said specifically *how* God will bless the other families of the earth through Abraham and his family, only that this is what God intends to do. Like many of the smaller Old Testament narratives, the entire story has to be understood with this as its heading, so that even where we go for many chapters and indeed whole books without any sense of a blessing coming upon the world through Israel, we should still understand that this is at least in the back of the writer's mind (albeit perhaps in the front of God's).

As I indicated, Genesis 3—11 offers a triple problem to which God's call to Abraham seems to be offered as the answer. Genesis 12 thus sends us back to Genesis 1—11 to ask, If this is the solution, what's the problem?

The tower of Babel. Working back from chapter 12, the first problem we encounter is the story of the tower of Babel (Genesis 11). Human arrogance reaches a height, quite literally, with the building of a tower to make a name and create security. God comes down to look at the puny little tower (the passage is full of ironic humor), and confuses human languages so that the human race won't be able to carry out its arrogant ambitions.

What is God doing about evil? On the one hand he is confronting it, judging it and doing something to stop it from having its desired effect. On the other hand he is doing something new, beginning a new project through which the underlying problem of the curse and the disunity of the human family will be replaced by blessing. How Abraham's family will reverse the curse of Babel is not clear; some would say it still isn't clear, as in the Middle East today Abraham's family is so firmly divided into two. This division, actually, goes back all the way to Genesis 16 and 21, with the birth first of Ishmael and then of Isaac, and leads right on to where we are today, with one branch of the family looking to Jerusalem and the other, at least in some modes, to Baghdad (ancient Babylon). When the promise of Genesis 12 comes through into the New Testament we discover its effect, of course, not least on the day of Pentecost. The question of how Pentecost is then to be applied to the problem posed in Genesis 11 is still a matter of urgent debate, to which we shall return.

We notice in particular two things. First, there is a link between the humans and the land. The arrogant people of Babel build a city and a tower; God calls Abraham to be a nomad—no fixed abode for a while yet—but promises him, eventually, a homeland. Second, we note that the "solution," or the answer, offered in Genesis 12 is strictly eschatological; that is, it lies in the future, and this means that the ongoing story from this point is bound to contain deep ambiguities. Abraham's family carries forward the promise of a future in which the world is put to rights, but it hasn't happened yet.

The result, to put it bluntly, is that Abraham's family will have its own local version of Babel. Ultimately, Abraham's family will go into exile, and the place of their exile is Babylon, Babel itself. The people of the solution will have to return to experience the problem.

The flood. Working back from Genesis 11, we come next to the story of the flood (Genesis 6—7), which contains one of the saddest lines in the whole of the Bible: God declares that the wickedness of the human race has grieved him to his heart, so much so that, as someone might say when in deep depression, he is sorry he ever made the world in the first place (Genesis 6:6).

The flood offers the same pattern of God's reaction to evil: on the one hand, a literally torrential judgment, blotting out both land and animals; on the other hand, an act of grace to rescue one family from the debacle, indicating both that God's purpose for creation will continue and that God is now committed to working out that purpose with sorrow and grief in his heart. Nothing in the story indicates that God thinks rescuing Noah and his family will somehow make them different, in their imagination and intentions, from the people of Genesis 6:5, whose wickedness was great, for whom every inclination of the thoughts of their hearts was only evil continually. Noah's family includes the people who build the tower of Babel as well as the family into which Abraham is born.

The flood stands as a reminder that God hates evil and what it does to his creation, that he can and sometimes will take steps to stop it in its tracks, but that—precisely because he is the sovereign Creator—he will find a way of working through and out the other side to fulfill the purpose which he still intends for creation. As with Babel, there is a close link between humans and the earth: the earth itself is flooded as part of God's judgment on the human race, and the sign of human rescue is the green olive shoot that comes up from the newly irrigated ground—significantly, brought to Noah by the dove, part of the nonhuman animal creation. The story ends in a vineyard, with the deeply mixed message both that a new fruitfulness has arrived and that new possibilities for evil will stalk the earth.

The forbidden fruit. Working back yet again, we come to the famous story in Genesis 3: the humans, the snake and the forbidden fruit. A great deal has been written on this, and I have no major new insights to offer into what is by any account one of the most profound, but also puzzling, stories in all literature. We all want to know what the story refuses to tell us: why there was a snake in God's beautiful creation in the first place, and why it wanted to use its cunning in that way. Instead of giving us an explanation for evil, the story gives us a brief analysis of it, not least the strong role of deception—of oneself and of others—and the way in which excuses come easily to the heart and tongue but can't put off the question of responsibility.

The narrative then tells us once more what God does about it. God judges the evil, with his judgment taking the form of expulsion from the garden and the imposition of a multiple curse. Humans must not be allowed to take fruit from the tree of life while they are in their rebellious condition; the ground itself is cursed and will produce sharp and obstructive weeds. God's project for creation must now proceed by a long and tortuous route, through thorns and thistles and dust and death.

Even in exile there are signs of blessing, though now mixed with almost equal signs of the curse. The original command, that

the humans should be fruitful and multiply, was not rescinded
even though it now carries a horrible ambiguity. Eve conceives
Cain with the help of the Lord, but he turns out in Genesis 4 to be
a murderer. The sign of God-given life carries within it the now
equally God-given curse of death. The refrain through the list of
Adam's descendants in Genesis 5—"and he died . . . and he
died"—reminds us over and over of what has happened in Genesis
3, even as new life in each generation brings new hope, until finally we reach Abraham and the fresh promise both of blessing
and of the land.

A new way. The great story which frames the Old Testament,
then, begins with this triple statement of the problem and of God's
repeated answer. Evil must be judged, and judged severely. God
has made a beautiful world; evil, insofar as we can define it at this
stage, is a defacing of that world, a way of getting the world upside
down and inside out.

Humans, instead of worshiping God as the source of their life,
give allegiance to the nonhuman creation. The earth, instead of being ruled wisely by God-fearing, image-bearing stewards, shares
the curse for the sake of idolatrous humankind. Death, which we
may rightly see as a natural and harmless feature of the original
landscape, now assumes the unwelcome guise of the executioner,
coming grimly to prevent the poison spreading too far. God's anxiety that Adam might now take fruit from the tree of life, and eat,
and live forever in his fallen state (Genesis 3:22) leads to God's
equal anxiety that arrogant humankind would be able to plot ever
greater and greater folly (Genesis 11:6). Judgment in the present

time is a matter of stopping evil in its tracks before it gets too far. The threatened "death" takes various forms: exile for Adam and Eve, the flood for Noah's generation, confusion and dispersal for Babel.

But God then declares in and through Abraham, as an act of sovereign grace following the word and act of judgment, that a new way has opened up by which the original purpose of blessing for humankind and creation can be taken forward. From within the story we already ought to perceive that this is going to be enormously costly for God himself. The loneliness of God looking for his partners, Adam and Eve, in the garden; the grief of God before the flood; the head-shaking exasperation of God at Babel—all these, God knows, he will have to continue to experience. And worse—there will be numerous further acts of judgment as well as mercy as the story unfolds. But unfold it will. The overarching picture is of the sovereign Creator God who will continue to work within his world until blessing replaces curse, homecoming replaces exile, olive branches appear after the flood and a new family is created in which the scattered languages can be reunited. That is the narrative which forms the outer frame for the canonical Old Testament.

PEOPLE OF THE SOLUTION, PEOPLE OF THE PROBLEM

From this point onward, the body of the Old Testament carries the deeply ambiguous story of Abraham's family—the people through whom God's solution was being taken forward, composed of people who were themselves part of the problem.

The narrator of Genesis leaves us in no doubt that Abraham

himself was far from being a plaster-cast saint. Twice he nearly throws the promises away by a self-protecting white lie about Sarah being his sister rather than his wife. He and Sarah then go about the business of children and inheritance in their own way rather than God's way; the result is the tragedy of Ishmael, sent into the wilderness with Hagar his mother, which leads directly to the nightmarish story of the near-sacrifice of Abraham and Sarah's own son, Isaac. Deeply complex though this latter story is, I am convinced that it is closely related to what Abraham and Sarah had done to Hagar and Ishmael. The promises will continue forward, but the promise-bearing people from Abraham on will know that it does so at a huge cost.

The story from Abraham to the Babylonian exile and beyond continues this theme, replete with its multiple ambiguities. Jacob cheats and lies his way into inheriting from his father Isaac, and then is himself cheated top to bottom by his father-in-law Laban. He returns to the Promised Land limping after his struggle with God, who keeps his promises but reminds his people as he does so of their own unworthiness and the surprising nature of grace. Jacob's sons sell their younger brother Joseph into slavery, where he learns, it seems, not only the humility he had previously lacked but also a strong sense of God's strange providence—the providence which is one of the Bible's central answers to "What does God do about evil?" When his brothers come in fear and trembling to see him after the death of their father Jacob, Joseph declares that "you intended evil against me, but God intended it for good" (Genesis 50:20).

Somehow, strangely (and to us sometimes even annoyingly), the Creator God will not simply abolish evil from his world. The question that swirls around these discussions is, Why not? We are not given an answer; we are instead informed in no uncertain terms that God will *contain* evil, that he will *restrain* it, that he will prevent it from doing its worst, and that he will even on occasion use the malice of human beings to further his own strange purposes.

The most deeply formative narrative in all Judaism, and one of the key biblical answers to the question of what God does with evil, is the story of the exodus, Israel's release from slavery in Egypt. Jacob's descendants have multiplied and become slaves in Egypt. The Egyptians are harsh and bullying taskmasters. God hears the cry of his people and comes to deliver them—not all at once and not by a single flash of lightning, but in what by now is emerging as a characteristic pattern, through the call of an individual, and then another individual to work alongside the first. These individuals are, as the story highlights, flawed and sometimes muddled human beings who themselves need to be rebuked and even punished, but who bear and articulate God's promise and his fresh, saving word of freedom.

The main judgment, though, falls on Egypt in the form of the plagues, resulting in Pharaoh's final dismissal of Israel, the crossing of the Red Sea and Israel's time in the wilderness. Forever afterward, to this day, one of the primary Jewish answers to the question, "What does God do with evil?" is that God judges the wicked pagans who are oppressing Israel, and he rescues his people from their grasp. That answer resonates through the whole Old Testament, not least in several of the Psalms, where the righteous sufferer pleads with God to defend his cause, his person and his life against the wicked, the oppressor and the ungodly. It comes through into the New Testament period in Jewish writings such as the Wisdom of Solomon.

The Old Testament itself makes it clear that this is only one side of the story, though it is the more encouraging one (unless you happen to be Pharaoh). The other side is that the Israel who is rescued is still a grumbling, rebellious, malcontented people. Instead of being grateful, obedient and trusting, as a naive reading of the exodus story might have led us to imagine, Israel spends forty years in the wilderness wanting to go back to Egypt, fearful of entering the Promised Land because there are giants there, and generally displaying all the signs of the fallen humanity to whose plight they were supposed to be the answer. The call to them on Sinai spoke of their being God's royal priesthood, a holy nation, his special people, a treasured possession out of all peoples (Exodus 19:5-6), but a group less like that would be hard to imagine.

The worst of it comes when, after a long description of the tabernacle to be built for God's worship and detailed instructions for the consecration of Aaron and his sons as priests to serve in it, we find Aaron himself making a golden calf and encouraging the people to worship it. Two thousand years later the rabbis would look back in sorrow and speak of that moment as the equivalent, in the story of Israel, of what Adam and Eve did in the garden. Israel was called to be God's promise-bearing people, the light to the nations, but Israel itself showed every sign of being in darkness.

What God did with evil then was once more to judge, and to do so with such severity that it looked as if he would have to start again from scratch with Moses as he had done with Noah. But God had made promises to Abraham, and as God was faithful to his purposes for the whole creation, so he would be faithful to his purposes for Abraham's family. And when Moses forcibly reminded God of this in one of the greatest prayers of the Bible (Exodus 32:11-14; 33:12-16), God remained faithful to the Israelites—even when they had been faithless to him.

Perhaps nowhere is the ambiguity of that position more poignant (with resonances that continue to this day) than in the conquest of Canaan. The story is told, like the Abraham stories are told, without any attempt to whitewash the failure and folly of Israel, even as they succeed in conquering most of the land. We have been prepared by the writer of Genesis for this moment (and for at least part of the moral problem it poses) as far back as Genesis 15: God tells Abraham that his descendants will come back to the Promised Land in the fourth generation because, he says, "the iniquity of the Amorites is not yet complete" (Genesis 15:16). The implication is that, running alongside or underneath the larger story of Abraham's family as God's means of dealing with evil in the world, there are subplots in which God is keeping an eye on the various nations of the world, not in order to punish them immediately if they are going to the bad, but in order to prevent their going beyond a certain limit. In Abraham's day, God knows that the Amorites are wicked, but it is clear that they will become more so. Sooner or later, at the appointed time, the non-Jewish peoples who occupy the land will be ripe for judgment, and then God will use his people and their entry to the land as the means of that judgment. This corresponds to the remarkable picture of God's moral providence we find in Isaiah 10:5-19, when God first uses the pagan arrogance of Assyria as a way of punishing rebellious Israel and then, when this work is complete, punishes Assyria in turn precisely for its pagan arrogance. This is presumably what the psalmist means (Psalm 76:10) by God turning human wrath to his praise.

This is a terrible responsibility for Israel, and Israel will not live up to it. Hence the tragicomic sequence of stories in the book of Judges when, after the conquest of the Promised Land under Joshua, the Israelites get it wrong over and over again, and God has to rescue them from scrape after scrape. The rescuers themselves, characteristically, are hardly pillars of virtue; think of the flawed hero Samson. We look back from our historical vantage point—and post-Enlightenment thought has looked back from its supposed position of moral superiority—and we shake our heads over the whole sorry business of conquest and settlement. Ethnic cleansing, we call it; however much the Israelites had suffered in Egypt, we find it hard to believe that they were justified in doing what they did to the Canaanites, or that the God who was involved in this operation was the same God we know in Jesus Christ.

And yet ever since the garden, ever since God's grief over Noah, ever since Babel and Abraham, the story has been about the messy way in which God has had to work to bring the world out of the mess. Somehow, in a way we are inclined to find offensive, God has to get his boots muddy and, it seems, to get his hands bloody, to put the world back to rights. If we declare, as many have done, that we would rather it were not so, we face a counter-question: Which bit of dry, clean ground are we standing on that we should pronounce on the matter with such certainty? Dietrich Bonhoeffer declared that the primal sin of humanity consisted in putting the knowledge of good and evil before the knowledge of God. That is one of the further dark mysteries of Genesis 3: there must be *some* substantial continuity between what we mean by good and evil and what God means; otherwise we are in moral darkness indeed. But it serves as a warning to us not to pontificate with too much certainty about what God should and shouldn't have done.

The stories of conquest conclude with Israel, the people of promise, embattled and rebellious but finally installed in the land. From then on, Israel is like a broken signpost still shakily pointing forward to the Creator's purpose: to rescue his human creatures and complete the work of creation.

The period of the judges gives way, with a sigh of relief on the part of the biblical book of Judges, to the period of the monarchy. But right from the start, as by now we should be expecting, the institution of the monarchy was itself flawed. The prophet Samuel knew that the people had asked for a king for the wrong reasons, and the first one God gave them (Saul) went bad. The next king, David—a man after God's own heart—was too interested (and then some!) in other people's wives; his own consequent experience of humiliating exile and almost equally humbling and costly restoration forms an advance pattern for the experience of the whole people five hundred years later.

It is quite clear on the one hand, particularly in the Psalms, that David and his dynasty are to be seen as God's answer to the problem of evil. They will bring judgment and justice to the world. Their dominion will be from one sea to the other, from the River to the ends of the earth. And yet the writers are all too aware of the puzzle and ambiguity of saying such a thing. The greatest royal psalm, Psalm 89, juxtaposes 37 verses of celebration of the wonderful things God will do through the Davidic king with 14 verses asking plaintively why it's all gone wrong. The psalm then ends with a single verse blessing YHWH forever. That is the classic Old Testament picture. Here are the promises; here is the problem; God remains sovereign over the paradox. Split the psalm up either way, and you fail to catch the flavor of the entire corpus of biblical writing. God's solution to the problem of evil, the establishment of the Davidic monarchy through which Israel will at last be the light to the nations, the bringer of justice to the world, comes already complete with a sense of puzzlement and failure, a sense that the plan isn't working in the way it should, that the only thing to do is to hold the spectacular promises in one hand and the messy reality in the other and praise YHWH anyway.

The Psalms indeed are a rich treasure house of reflection on evil and what God does with it, as indeed of so much else. The Psalter opens with a classic statement of one part of Jewish belief: People who walk in the way of YHWH are blessed, while the wicked will be like the chaff which the wind blows away. This conventional wisdom is repeated frequently in other psalms and of course in Proverbs too. One psalm even risks life and limb and declares (Psalm 37:25) that, though the writer has been young and now is old, he has never seen the righteous forsaken or their seed begging for bread.

We don't need to look at the book of Job to find out that things aren't always that straightforward. Several other psalms come quickly, almost angrily, to point out that the righteous suffer injustice and God doesn't seem to do anything about it. Psalm 73 forms one of the towering statements of this, wrestling with the problem and pointing at last toward a long-term solution: God will act in the end, perhaps beyond death itself, to judge the wicked and vindicate the righteous. Psalm 94 goes in a similar direction: the present sufferings of the righteous are to be seen as divine chastisement leading to eventual rescue and salvation, while the wicked will have their sufferings kept in reserve for later, for ultimate punishment. Several psalms ask "How long, O Lord?" and by no means receive an unambiguous answer. And sandwiched between the lovely little poem we know as "Glorious Things of Thee Are Spoken" and the royal Psalm 89, we have Psalm 88, the darkest and most hopeless of any prayer in Scripture:

> Wretched and close to death from my youth up,
> I suffer your terrors; I am desperate.
> Your wrath has swept over me;
> your dread assaults destroy me.
> They surround me like a flood all day long;
> from all sides they close in on me.

You have caused friend and neighbor to shun me;

And darkness is my only companion. (Psalm 88:15-18)

The only note of hope here (if indeed it is that) is the second person singular. The psalmist will not suggest that what is happening to him is other than the strange and terrifying work of YHWH himself. He can't understand it; he knows it isn't what ought to be happening; but he holds on, almost one might think to the point of blasphemy, to the belief that YHWH remains sovereign.

This, of course, is what happens with the prophets of the exile, and indeed Psalm 88 might be read as a corporate statement corresponding to the Lamentations of Jeremiah. Though the pagan nations celebrate their triumph not only over Israel but over Israel's God, the prophets of the time insist that YHWH himself has done to Israel what he had done to Adam and Eve so long before: expelling them from the land, the promised garden, because of their rebellion. The story of exile and restoration so central to the Bible becomes the great and mysterious answer to the question, "What does YHWH do about evil?" The question of God's justice, raised implicitly all over the Bible, is here faced head on.

This is where, in the third and last main section of this chapter, we reach the three books that invite us higher up the mountain—even if it means going into the mist—to listen for fresh words of wisdom.

MY SERVANT ISRAEL, MY SERVANT JOB

"Have you considered," asks God to Satan, "my servant Job?" Well, Satan had and he hadn't, and part of the puzzle of Job is why God put the question like that to Satan in the first place. But before we consider Job for ourselves, I want to look at the other great Servant of YHWH in the Old Testament—if indeed he is that different from Job—and then at another book in which a similar pattern is worked out.

Isaiah 40—55. The book in the Old Testament having, on its surface, the most to do with God's justice or righteousness is chapters 40—55 (or perhaps 40—66) of the book of the prophet Isaiah, sometimes called Second Isaiah.

Isaiah 40—55, commonly supposed to date from the time of the exile (though nothing for my purpose hinges on this), wrestles with the question of how YHWH can be righteous, granted that Israel is condemned to exile. It quickly emerges that this is the focal point, at the smaller, close-up level, of the problem of God's moral governance of the world as a whole. Israel in exile in Babylon is like Adam and Eve expelled from the garden. But God had created the human race as his image-bearing stewards to rule wisely on his behalf over creation, and that covenant is not forgotten. That is the biblical shape of the problem of evil: the long memory of the human task under God is currently in tension with the fact that humans have rebelled and that the ground bears thorns and thistles.

Similarly, Israel has been exiled for gross misconduct: idolatry, immorality, persistent refusal to hear YHWH calling her back to obedience. But God has called Israel to be the people through whom he will redeem the world, humankind and creation itself, and that intention is not forgotten. The larger biblical shape of the problem of evil is reflected in the more sharply focused shape of the problem of Israel in exile. Isaiah 40—55 proclaims that YHWH is still the sovereign creator, that he is still in covenant with Israel, that he is above all righteous *(tzaddik)*. Because of this righteousness, this faithfulness both to covenant and to creation, Israel will be rescued and creation itself will be restored. Isaiah 55, the magnificent climax of the whole section, glories in the fact that the thorn will be replaced by the cypress and the brier with the myrtle. The curse of Genesis 3 itself, along with the subsequent curses on Israel (as, for instance, in Isaiah 5) will be undone when Israel is redeemed and the covenant reestablished.

If you want to understand God's justice in an unjust world, says the prophet, this is where you must look. God's justice is not simply a blind dispensing of rewards for the virtuous and punishments for the wicked, though plenty of those are to be found on the way. God's justice is a saving, healing, restorative justice, because the God to whom justice belongs is the Creator God who has yet to complete his original plan for creation and whose justice is designed not simply to restore balance to a world out of kilter but to bring to glorious completion and fruition the creation, teeming with life and possibility, that he made in the first place. And he remains implacably determined to complete this project through his image-bearing human creatures and, more specifically, through the family of Abraham.

But how? Woven closely into the fabric of Isaiah 40—55 stands the figure of the Servant: YHWH's Servant, the one through whom YHWH's purpose of justice and salvation will be carried out. The Servant comes before us in Isaiah 42 as a royal figure, clearly

linked to the royal figure in chapters 9 and 11 of Isaiah, and the
similar one in Isaiah 61; yet he is in many ways quite unlike a king.
He is clearly Israel, or perhaps we should say Israel-in-person,
sharing the vocation of Israel and now sharing the fate of Israel,
exiled, crushed, and killed. And yet he also stands over against Israel, so that Israel itself looks on in horror at his fate; even the remnant within Israel is described as "those who hear the Servant's
voice." Somehow Isaiah has so redefined the broader problem of
evil—the injustice of the world and the justice of the one Creator
God—so that we now see it not as a philosopher's puzzle requiring
explanation but as the tragedy of all creation requiring a fresh act
from the sovereign Creator God.

To our amazement and (if we know what we are about) horror,
we discover in Isaiah 53 that this fresh act comes into sharp focus
in the suffering and death of the Servant himself. Sharing the fate
of Israel in the exile which, as we know from Genesis 3 onward, is
closely aligned with death itself, he bears the sin of the many. He
embodies the covenant faithfulness, the restorative justice, of the
sovereign God; and with his stripes "we" (presumably the "we" of
the remnant, looking on in wonder and fear) are healed.

Central to the Old Testament picture of God's justice in an unjust world, then, is the picture of God's faithfulness to unfaithful
Israel. And central to that picture is the picture of YHWH's Servant, an individual who stands over against Israel and takes Israel's
fate upon himself so that Israel may be rescued from exile, allowing the human race at last to proceed, as in Isaiah 55, toward the
new creation, in which thorns and thistles will be replaced by cy-

press and myrtle, dust and death by fresh water and new life. The greatest prophet of the Old Testament points forward, without further explanation, to a fresh act of the one true God in which this will be accomplished. The Servant is both Israel and God's fresh emissary to Israel; he is both the king and the one who does what no king could ever do. As far as the Old Testament is concerned, all this remains a puzzle—the positive side of the puzzle of evil itself.

The book of Daniel. A similar puzzle is found in the second of the three books I draw on at this point, one of the first writings to apply Isaiah 40—55 to subsequent situations. The book of Daniel is all about the problem of evil: pagan empires do their worst, and the one true God acts in judgment on them and in vindication of his true people. At various points in the book, but particularly in Daniel 11—12, the servant figure seems to be applied to the righteous within Israel, those who stay loyal to YHWH even in exile and suffer for it, those who are martyred at the hands of a pagan empire, those who are (in the book's central image; see my chapter one) mauled by the monsters who come up from the sea. The kingdoms of the world rage against the kingdom of God; the problem of evil grows teeth and claws, leaping out with a snarl from the debating halls of the philosophers and onto the stage of the real world, turning gardens into deserts and human lives to dust and ashes.

As I argued in the last chapter, one of the reasons our contemporary world has not been able to come to terms with the reality of evil, and has instead reacted to it in immature and inappropriate ways, is because it has thought of evil either as a philosopher's puzzle at which secularism has long shrugged its shoulders or as an old-fashioned difficulty which modernity has at last solved. Those on the one hand who study Daniel, and those who study the real contemporary world on the other, ought to know better. Evil is alive and powerful, not least where mighty empires vaunt themselves and imagine they can do as they please.

At the center of the book of Daniel, corresponding in some ways to the figure of the Servant in Isaiah and fulfilling a similar role in terms of both receiving and embodying the saving justice of God, is the figure of "one like a Son of Man" (Daniel 7:13). The original meaning and subsequent understandings of this phrase are highly controversial, and I have written at some length about them elsewhere. But the drama of Daniel 7 is not to be collapsed into mere linguistic debates. The monsters that come up from the sea, as we saw, make war against the human figure; but God exalts the human one over the beasts.

This is at one level much like Adam in the garden being set in authority over the animals. That, indeed, is part of the point: this is an image of creation restored, put back into proper working order. But this time, after the long history of evil and of creation out of joint, the animals are threatening, and the newly reestablished human rule over them is one of punitive judgment. Daniel 7 is basically a court scene: God takes his seat, and judgment is given for the human against the beasts. This is what God's justice over the unjust world will look like. God's restoration of creation must come about through his proper overthrow of the forces of evil and his vindication of his faithful people. The questions we are left with at the end of Daniel are: Who are God's faithful people? How will it all work out? Who is this Son of Man?

The book of Job. The third and final book to be considered (far too briefly, inevitably) is of course the noble and deeply puzzling book of Job. Out of the many things that could and perhaps should be said at this point, I choose the following six.

First, the book of Job, like some of the psalms, raises the question of the moral providence of God in the light of rampant evil—in this case, evil directed against Job himself. The question of God's justice is pointed out by the book of Job in a manner parallel to the way it is raised in the literature of the exile; the answer, if it is an answer, consists of a fresh display of the power of God as Creator, which is the theological basis also of the answers, if they are answers, offered by Isaiah and Daniel.

Second, whereas Israel was—and the prophets like Isaiah, Jeremiah, Ezekiel and Daniel insist loudly on this point—emphatically guilty, the whole point of the book of Job is that Job was innocent. The normal analysis of the exile was that Israel thoroughly deserved it; the whole point of Job is that Job didn't. His comforters, relying no doubt on a simplistic reading of Deuteronomy, Psalm 1 and so on, insist that good people have good things happen to them and bad people have bad things; therefore, if bad things happen to you, you must have done something wrong. The book of Job enters a massive protest against this as a blanket analysis of how things are in the present world. It is like Psalm 73 except that its stridency is far longer drawn out and without the same kind of resolution.

Third, the book is framed by the opening two chapters, in which we learn both that "the satan" is the source of Job's problem and that God has given him permission—we might almost say encouragement—to do what he has done. This is one of the rare occasions when "the satan" puts in an appearance in the Old Testament (the main other one being the account of David's census in 1 Chronicles 21:1). It's clear that the word *satan* is a title, an office: he is "the accuser," the director of public prosecutions. He doesn't exactly tempt Job to sin, though perhaps part of the point is that he's tempting him to curse God, and Job refuses. (He curses everything else, including the day he was born, but he simply complains to God and asks what's happened to his celebrated divine justice.) We are invited, in other words, to look at Job's torment and his questions with the privileged knowledge that this is not in fact a contest between Job and God, as Job (who, knowing himself to be innocent, thinks that God has made a terrible blunder) and his would-be comforters (who, confident that God doesn't make mistakes, assume that Job must somehow be guilty) think it is. It is also not—or not straightforwardly—a contest between God and Satan, as a dualist might imagine. No, it is a contest between Satan and Job. Satan is trying to get Job in his power, to demonstrate that humans are not worth God's trouble, while Job for his part continues to insist both that God ought to be just and that he himself is in the right.

Fourth, the majestic display of the created order which forms the denouement of the book (Job 38—41) both is and isn't an answer to the problem. Indeed in one sense it restates the problem: if God really is the sovereign Creator, ruling Behemoth and Leviathan and calling the north wind out of its shed, then he ought to do a better job of running the moral side of the cosmos. Neither is Job 38—41 simply a way of saying, "I'm God, and I'm very powerful, so you just shut up." Nor do I think it's likely, despite a recent scholarly suggestion, that Behemoth and Leviathan are intended as *evil* creatures over whom God is displaying his sovereignty. Within the larger canonical context, it ought to be clear that reemphasizing the doctrine of creation is indeed the foundation of all biblical answers to questions about who God is and what he's doing. This is so, as we've seen, both for Isaiah and for Daniel, and it remains so in the New Testament.

Fifth, and perhaps most important, the conclusion to the book in Job 42, which many have felt to be a letdown almost to the point of bathos, is important for what it insists on. It might have been easy for the author, if he had been of a different theological position, to say that after Job's death the angels carried him to a paradise where everything was so wonderful that he forgot the terrible time he'd had on earth. But that is emphatically not the point. The question is about God's moral government of *this* world, not about the way in which we should leave this world behind and find consolation in a different one. That is the high road to Buddhism, not to biblical theology. We may find the last chapter of the book a bit trivial, and it does seem to leave the writer still open to Dostoyevsky's question in *The Brothers Karamazov* about whether it's possible for God to justify himself in the face of the torture of a single child. But it insists that if God is the Creator (and that, after all, is the premise of the whole book), then it matters that things be put right within creation itself, not somewhere else.

Sixth (pointing ahead to my next chapter), the parallel between Job and YHWH's Servant in Isaiah remains striking. The Servant is innocent, after all, just as Job is. He doesn't complain, as Job does, yet he too suffers indignity, pain and despair. To look once again at the larger context of the whole canon of Scripture, there may be something to be said for seeing the book of Job as an anticipation of the harrowing scene in Gethsemane, where the comforters again fail and creation itself goes dark as the monsters close in around the innocent figure who is asking what it's all about. But more of that in the next chapter. The book of Job remains, in its own terms, as a monument not only to astonishing literary skill but to the theological pursuit of answers that refuse to be put off, the theological insistence that to "solve" the problem of evil in the present age is to belittle it, and the theological celebration, in the teeth of the apparent evidence, of Israel's God as Creator and Lord of the world.

CONCLUSION

There are literally dozens of things that could be said to conclude this whirlwind tour of the Old Testament's way of approaching the problem of evil, but I confine myself to four, the last of which opens up just a little further.

First, the personified force of evil, the satan, is important but not that important. The origin of evil itself remains a mystery; and the satan, when he (or it) appears, is kept strictly within bounds. We are still some way from the dragon of Revelation or even from the sinister figure whispering in Jesus' ear on the Mount of Temptation.

Second, human responsibility for evil is clear throughout. And though no theory of this is offered, all humans appear to share in the problem—or virtually all; Ezekiel 14:14 lists Noah, Daniel and Job as the three most righteous men who ever lived, and we remind ourselves of Noah's drunkenness, Daniel's prayer of confession and Job's hand across his mouth with nothing more to say in his own defense. Abraham got it wrong; so, sometimes, did Moses; David, a great saint, was also a great sinner; and so on. God chooses to bring the world back to rights through a family which is itself composed of deeply flawed human beings and thereby generates second- and third-order problems of evil—which have to be addressed and solved in their turn. Only the strange, silent figure of Isaiah 53 stands before us as one who, it is said, remains innocent and righteous.

Third, the evil that humans do is integrated with the enslavement of creation. This is seldom a matter of one-on-one cause and effect, but there is a nexus, a web of rippling events that spreads out from human rebellion against the Creator to the out-of-jointness of creation itself. In the same way, when humans are put back to rights, the world will be put back to rights. No theory is offered about earthquakes or other so-called natural disasters, though no doubt the prophets would have been happy to identify them as heaven-sent warnings.

Fourth, the Old Testament never tries to give us the sort of picture the philosophers want, that of a static world order with everything explained tidily. At no point does the picture collapse into the simplistic one which so many skeptics assume must be what religious people believe, in which God is the omnicompetent managing director of a very large machine and ought to be able to keep it in proper working order. What we are offered instead is stranger and more mysterious: a narrative of God's project of justice within a world of injustice.

This project is a matter of setting the existing creation to rights rather than scrapping it and doing something else instead. God decides, for that reason, to work through human beings as they are—even though their hearts think only of evil—and through Israel, even though from Abraham onward they make as many mistakes as they do acts of obedience. Both in the grand narrative itself, and in many smaller moments within it, we observe a pattern of divine action, to judge and punish evil and to set bounds to it without destroying the responsibility and agency of human beings themselves; and also both to promise and to bring about new moments of grace, events which constitute new creation, however much they are themselves necessarily shot through with ambiguity.

This is not, I think, exactly the same as the "free-will defense," beloved by some who try to explain or vindicate God ("God gave us free will so it's all our fault"). It is more a "commitment to action" on God's part, coupled with the settled affirmation of creation as still basically good. God cannot undo that good creation even though it has gone wrong. He will therefore act from *within* the world he has created, affirming that world in its created otherness even as he is putting it to rights.

Within this fourth point we find, at least in pattern and outline, the signposts that will lead us, however obliquely and ambiguously, to that narrative which offers itself as the climax of the Old Testament. The moment when the sinfulness of humankind grieved God to his heart, the moment when the Servant was despised and rejected, the moment when Job asked God why it had to be that way, came together when the Son of Man knelt, lonely and afraid, before going to face the might of the beasts that had at last come up out of the sea. The story of Gethsemane and of the crucifixion of Jesus of Nazareth present themselves in the New Testament as the strange, dark conclusion to the story of what God does about evil, of what happens to God's justice when it takes human flesh, when it gets its feet muddy in the garden and its hands bloody on the cross. The multiple ambiguities of God's actions in the world come together in the story of Jesus, the story that will be the subject of the next chapter.

EVIL AND THE CRUCIFIED GOD

Why did Jesus die? Many reasons could be given: the Romans were concerned that he might pose a security threat; the Jewish authorities were upset at his action in the temple; his disciples let him down; Jesus himself believed, in some sense, that it was his vocation. I have explored all this much more fully in chapter twelve of *Jesus and the Victory of God*.

But when we ask the question, Why did Jesus die? with an eye to the deeper issue of why, *in the purposes of God*, Jesus might have had to die, we move from historical analysis of events and motivations to a theological account of what God decided to do about evil. That, ultimately, is what theories of "the atonement" are all about. And in order to address the question like that, it is naturally necessary to have some idea of what "evil" itself might be. This is, in the nature of the case, a two-way street: it isn't just that you come with a view of evil and then design a doctrine of the atonement to show how God has answered this problem, though no doubt some have done that. There are clear signs from the New Testament onward that Christian theologians have often, perhaps even usually, gazed in awe, horror and gratitude on the crucifixion of Jesus and have deduced from that something profound about the nature of evil. "If righteousness could come by the law," wrote Paul, "the Messiah's death would not have been necessary" (Galatians 2:21).

In the opening chapter, I argued that evil is real and powerful, that it is more than the sum total of individual sin, and that it cannot be properly understood through dualism, whether the ontological dualism that sees the created world as evil and the solution as being to escape it, or the sociological dualism that divides the world into "us" (good) and "them" (bad). Then, in the second chapter, I presented a reading of the Old Testament in which I argued that the entire canon—not just key passages like the book of Job—tells a story which, from a bewildering variety of angles, is all about what God (the Creator God, please note) is doing about evil. God has undertaken a plan: it is a daring and risky plan, involving God in so much ambiguity—one might almost say subterfuge—that he begins to look like a double agent, becoming compromised at many points in order to pull off the solution. This plan involves drawing evil to a point in order to deal with it there. The Old Testament symbols which speak of God's strategy for dealing with evil include the temple, where the regular sacrifices were a constant reminder of both sin and grace, and human kings, priests and prophets—particularly, as we saw, the figures of the Servant and the Son of Man, both of whom emerge at the point where Israel, the people who carry God's promise to deal with the world's evil, is itself overwhelmed by the weight and force of evil itself.

All this leads to an initial reflection. Theologies of the cross, of how God deals with sin through the death of Jesus, have not normally grappled with the larger problem of evil as I set it out in the first chapter. Conversely, most people who have written about "the problem of evil" within philosophical theology have not normally grappled sufficiently with the cross as part of both the analysis and the solution of that problem. The two have been held apart, in a mismatch, with "the problem of evil" on the one hand being conceived simply in terms of "How could a good and powerful God allow evil into the world in the first place?" and the atonement on the other hand being seen in terms simply of personal forgiveness, of the various categories set out movingly (if ultimately inadequately) in the hymn "There Is a Green Hill Far Away," successive verses of which run through the various ways of saying what a personalized "atonement" wants to say:

> He died that we might be forgiven,
> He died to make us good,
> That we might go at last to Heaven,
> Saved by His precious blood.

Much nineteenth- and twentieth-century Christian thought has accepted the framework offered by the Enlightenment, in which the Christian faith has the role of rescuing people from the evil world, ensuring them forgiveness in the present and heaven hereafter. The Enlightenment-based wider world has then accepted that evaluation of the Christian faith—not surprisingly, since it was driving it in the first place—and so has not thought it necessary to factor Christian theology into its own discussions of "the problem of evil." How, after all, does a hymn like "There Is a Green Hill Far Away" have anything at all to say to a world dumbstruck in horror at World War I, at Auschwitz, at Hiroshima, at September 11, 2001? And even if theologians like Jürgen Moltmann have made a start putting back together what ought not to have been split apart, we are still left with what seems a huge uphill task.

REREADING THE GOSPELS

At this point, what we need is to reread the Gospels as what they are, not as what they are not. It often appears—as I know only too well from my years of teaching and examining students within a university world where the dominant paradigm was still at work—that there is not actually that much "atonement theology" in the Gospels. Mark's "theology of the cross" often seemed to be reduced to one key verse, Mark 10:45, which evokes Isaiah 53 in speaking of the Son of Man coming "to give his life as a ransom for many" *(lutron anti pollōn)*. Luke, who seemed to have deliberately avoided following Mark at that point, was often held therefore to have drawn back from offering any real atonement theology. The Lord's Supper gave hints towards an atonement theology, and the crucifixion narratives, especially in their evocation of biblical allusions, provided some further elements. But for the most part the Gospels, as read within the mainstream tradition both of scholarship and of church life—and I mean the life of the churches that might be expected to be on the lookout for atonement theology and to exploit it where it was to be found—had little to contribute, except as a general narrative backcloth to a theology of atonement grounded in Paul, Hebrews and 1 Peter.

When, however, we read the Gospels in the holistic fashion in which, arguably, they ask to be read, we find that they tell a double story, in which the themes of my first two chapters are drawn together into a single point. The Gospels tell the story of how the evil in the world—political, social, personal, moral, emotional—reached its height, and how God's long-term plan for Israel (and for himself!) finally came to its climax. They tell both of these stories in—and as—the story of how Jesus of Nazareth announced God's kingdom and went to his violent death.

In this chapter, I shall unpack this dense statement, and then show how the Gospels, read in this way, offer us both a richer theology of atonement than we are used to and also a deeper understanding of the problem of evil itself and what must be done about it in our own day.

1. The Gospels tell the story of the *political* powers of the world reaching their full, arrogant height. All early readers of the Gospels knew perfectly well that the word *gospel* itself—never mind any teaching about "God's kingdom"—was a direct confrontation with the regime of Caesar, the news of whose rule was referred to in his empire as "good news," "gospel." Rome stands in the shadowy

background of all the Gospel stories, and when at last Jesus meets
the Roman governor Pilate, the shrewd reader has a sense of denouement, the unveiling of the real confrontation that has been
taking place all along. Similarly (a point we see particularly in Matthew's Gospel), the presence of the house of Herod and the story
of John the Baptist offer constant reminders that the local Jewish
(or would-be Jewish) pseudo-aristocracy did not take kindly to
the presence or proclamation of an alternative "king of the Jews."
Finally, the corrupt Jerusalem regime of Caiaphas and his high
priestly house, who again come on stage only at the climax of the
story, are part of the deep structure of the problem, as human systems overreach themselves from every angle and end up putting
Jesus on the cross.

2. The Gospels thus also tell the story of *corruption within Israel
itself*, as the people who bear the solution have themselves become
(with terrible irony that causes Paul to weep every time he thinks
of it) a central part of the problem. The Pharisees are offering an
interpretation of Torah which pursues a kind of holiness but only
makes matters worse. The priests in the temple are offering the
sacrifices which should speak of God's grace but which instead
speak of their own exclusive and corrupt system. The revolutionaries try to get in on the act of God's in-breaking kingdom (Matthew 11:12), but their attempt to fight violence with violence can
only ever result in a victory *for* violence, not a victory over it. This
means that the death of Jesus, when it comes, is bound to be seen
as the work not only of the pagan nations but of the Israel that has
longed, as (with further irony) on the day when it chose a king in

the first place, to become "like all the nations" (1 Samuel 8:5, 20) and now is reduced to saying that it has no king but Caesar (John 19:15).

3. The Gospels then tell the story of the deeper, darker forces which operate *at a suprapersonal level,* forces for which the language of the demonic, despite all its problems, is still at the least inadequate. These forces of evil operate within all of the human elements just described but cannot be reduced simply to their terms. The Gospels introduce us to "the satan," the quasi-personal "accuser" which is doing its best to drag Jesus down into the trap into which Israel, like the rest of the world, has already fallen. The shrieking demons that yell at him as he performs healings, that rush at him out of the tombs, are signs that a battle has been joined at a more than merely personal level. The dark, stormy sea evokes ancient Israelite imagery of an evil which is more than the sum total of present wrongdoing and woe. "The power of darkness" to which Jesus alludes immediately before his betrayal (Luke 22:53) indicates an awareness that on that night in particular evil was being given a scope, a free rein, to do its worst in ways for which the soldiers, the betrayer, the muddled disciples and the corrupt court were merely long-range outworkings. The mocking of the bystanders as Jesus hangs on the cross ("If you are the son of God . . .") echoes the taunting, tempting voice that had whispered in the desert. The power of death itself, the ultimate denial of the goodness of creation, speaks of a force of destruction, of anti-world, anti-God power being allowed to do its worst. The Gospels tell this whole story in order to say that the tortured

young Jewish prophet hanging on the cross was the point where evil had become truly and fully and totally itself.

4. The Gospels tell the story of Jesus as a story in which the line between good and evil runs not between Jesus and his friends on the one hand and everyone else on the other—certainly not between Jews and Gentiles—but *down the middle of Jesus' followers themselves.* Peter, called to be the rock, is immediately denounced as "Satan." Thomas grumbles and doubts. James and John want the best seats in the kingdom. All of them argue about who will get the top jobs. Judas is Judas is Judas, the deepest enigma of all. In any case, once swords begin to flash in the garden torchlight, loyalty and courage desert them, and they in turn desert Jesus. We could perhaps make a case for some of the women in the Gospels being loyal and devoted while the men fall apart, but it would be largely an argument from silence. Granted the situation in which the Gospels were being written up, the candor with which the failings of the church's first leaders are described is remarkable.

5. The story the Gospels tell is a story about the *downward spiral* of evil. One thing leads to another; the remedy offered against evil has itself the germ of evil within it, so that its attempt to put things right merely produces second-order evil, and so on. Judas's betrayal and Peter's denial are simply among the last twists of this story, with the casual injustice of Caiaphas the high priest and Pilate the governor and the mocking of the crowds at the cross tying all the ends together.

These five points lead us to say that the story the Gospels are trying to tell us is the story of how the death of Jesus is the point at which evil in all its forms has come rushing together. Jesus' death is the result both of the major political evil of the world, the power games which the world was playing as it still does, *and* of the dark, accusing forces which stand behind those human and societal structures, forces which accuse creation itself of being evil, and so try to destroy it while its Creator is longing to redeem it. The Gospels tell the story of Jesus' death as the story of how the downward spiral of evil finally hit bottom with the violent and bloody execution of this man, this prophet who had announced God's kingdom. And if this is the way the Gospels are telling the story of Jesus, what conclusion do the writers want us to draw?

JESUS DEALING WITH EVIL

We might stop at this point and say, "Very well, the Gospels tell us that evil, as we have analyzed it already, was indeed the cause of Jesus' death; but by itself this would not constitute a *solution* to the problem of evil but simply a *restatement* of it." We cannot simply say, "Yes, evil put Jesus on the cross, but the resurrection reversed all that." The Gospels tell a deeper, more complex story by far. This is where the second strand comes in: the Gospels are *also* the story of how God's long-term plan from Abraham through to the time of Jesus, the apparently ambiguous and risky plan which we explored in chapter two, finally came to fruition. We can see this close-up in the way the Gospels tell the stories of Jesus during his public career. I have written about this at length in various places (notably *The Challenge of Jesus* and chapters five through ten of *Jesus and the Victory of God*); I simply summarize them here.

Jesus' healings. Jesus reaches out and touches the leper. Somehow, instead of the infection being passed to him, his wholeness, his "cleanness," is transmitted to the leper instead. Jesus allows himself to be touched by the woman with the issue of blood, whose every touch would render someone else unclean; but power flows instead from him to her, and she is healed. He touches the corpse of the widow's son at Nain, and instead of Jesus contracting uncleanness, the corpse comes back to life.

The Gospel writers intend us, I believe, to see the same phenomenon at work all the way to the cross. There Jesus at last identifies himself with the Jewish revolutionaries in their failing cause, to bring the kingdom for which they had longed but in the way they had refused.

Jesus' table fellowship with sinners. Jesus celebrates the kingdom with all the wrong people. He incurs anger and hostility from those who knew in their bones that God's kingdom was about holiness and detachment from evil, and who never suspected that evil people could be, and were being, redeemed and rescued. His mother and brothers come to take him away, thinking him to be out of his mind, and he responds by declaring that the crowd around him, hanging on his every word, were his mother and brothers. He tells stories (a lost sheep, a lost coin, two lost sons) to indicate for those with ears to hear that this policy was not an accident but a heaven-sent priority. He invites himself to lunch with Zacchaeus the Jericho tax collector while the crowds wait, shocked to the core, outside the door: "He's gone in to eat with a sinner!" Finally, he goes out to die with the rebels, sharing their shame though himself innocent, as Luke in particular makes clear. The taint of evil lies heavy on him throughout, and somehow he bears it, takes it all the way, exhausts its power.

Jesus articulates and models the call to Israel to be Israel. Jesus expresses God's call in a new way in the summons he issues to his followers. Israel is to be at last the light of the world, the city set on a hill. Israel is to show the world what it means to be God's people, God's servant-folk for the world: turn the other cheek, go the second mile, don't resist the pagans who want to take you for all you've got. Then, with those deeply challenging sayings from the Sermon on the Mount ringing in our ears, we read on in Matthew's Gospel to observe the Son of Man bringing God's judgment to the world, putting the world to rights, winning victories over evil, declaring forgiveness of sins on his own authority, announcing that he has the right to suspend sabbath regulations. Then we observe the Messiah coming into his kingdom, winning the real battle, cleansing the temple, bringing God's rule to the world as Psalm 2 had said he would, but doing so in a way previously unimagined. Then, finally, we watch the Son of Man, the Messiah, as he takes on himself the role of the Servant, the ultimate representative of Israel, bearing the sin and shame of Israel and so of the world. And as the story winds to its violent conclusion, we realize with a start that he has been obedient to the Israel-vocation which he had himself announced in the bracing and so often misunderstood Sermon on the Mount. He had turned the other cheek. He had picked up the Roman cross and gone the second mile. He was set up on the hill, unable to be hidden. He was acting as Israel, the light of the world, on behalf of the Israel that had embraced the pagan darkness. Mark 10:45 (with its parallel in Matthew 20:28) is not, after all, an isolated or detached statement of theological interpretation superimposed on an otherwise bare and theologically neutral narrative. It is the tip of the iceberg which tells us what is under the surface, down to the depths.

We could summarize the theme, deeply embedded as it is in the Gospel stories, in the following fashion:

1. Jesus had warned his people of God's impending judgment for their failure to follow his call to be the light of the world, for their failure to embody within their own life that justice and mercy to which God had called them.

2. Jesus had identified totally with Israel (as the Messiah, the Servant, was bound to do): taking its vocation upon himself, coming to the point of pain, of uncleanness, of sickness, folly, rebellion and sin.

3. Jesus was thus taking on himself the direct consequences, in the political and in the theological realm alike, of the failure and sin of Israel. He was dying, quite literally, for their sins. (I once saw a bumper sticker beside an Indian reservation on the shores of the Ottawa river to the west of Montreal, declaring that "Custer died for your sins." That was making a very similar point.) This is not a piece of strange or arbitrary theology read into the narrative at a later stage. This, the Gospels are telling us, is what it was all about all along. Jesus was taking upon himself the direct result of the ways in which God's people had failed in their vocation.

In particular, Matthew, Mark, Luke and John are declaring, each in their very different ways, that all this was simultaneously Jesus' own intention (in a vocation whose roots went deep into the Old Testament and into his personality, formed in prayer and study from boyhood and confirmed dramatically at his baptism) and the intention of God himself. Israel's God had long promised that he would return to Jerusalem to rule, to judge, to heal and to save. Now he was coming to the city at last with all of that in mind, telling stories about the king who had promised to come back, warning of the consequences of not being ready. He was the hen who longed to gather the chickens under his protective wings. He was the green tree, the only one with life within him, while all around were dry, dead branches ready for burning.

In particular, Jesus had made his own dark theme with deep biblical roots. There would come a time of great suffering, great tribulation, and only by passing through that time would God's promised rescue come. Jesus came to believe, in that kind of vocation at which one can only stand amazed and awed, that the *peirasmos*, the great "time of testing" of which prophets and oracles had spoken, was about to burst upon the world like a great tidal wave, and he had to take its full force upon himself so that everyone else could be spared. "Keep awake and pray," he said to his followers in the garden, "that you may not come into the *peirasmos*" (Mark 14:38); if all he meant was the general advice that after a good meal with rich wines one should say one's prayers lest one be tempted to commit some everyday sin, the scene would be reduced to bathos, almost to farce. No, the great, dark, horrible power of evil was bearing down on him, and Jesus had long realized that as Israel's representative he, and he alone, had the task to do what, according to the same Scriptures, Israel's God had said that he and he alone could do. He knelt there, a mile or so from the Gehenna he had predicted as the city's smoldering fate, believing that he had to go ahead, to stand in the breach, to take that fate upon himself. There is no way around this extraordinary, breathtaking combination of theological, personal, cosmic themes. The only way of doing justice to what the Gospels are trying to tell us is to grasp the picture in its entirety.

EARLY CHRISTIAN VIEW OF EVIL'S DEFEAT

Two reflections emerge from all this which constitute, at one and the same time, the foundation of early Christian atonement-theology and the start of the New Testament's answer to the problem of evil.

1. Paul saw, in his dramatic statement in Romans 7:1—8:11, that in the death of Jesus God had condemned sin, passed and executed judicial sentence upon it (Romans 8:3). God's great *No* to evil had been acted out in the person of Jesus, the person who could and did represent Israel as its Messiah, and hence the person who represented the whole world.

2. The New Testament writers report in various ways the remarkable sign of evil doing its worst and being exhausted. When Jesus suffered, he did not curse, and when he was reviled, he did not revile in return (1 Peter 2:23). "Father, forgive them" (Luke 23:34): that constitutes a radical innovation in the long and noble tradition of Jewish martyr stories, where (as, for instance, in 2 Mac-

cabees 7) the heroes, while being tortured to death, call down God's vengeance on their persecutors and warn them of coming judgment.

The immediate result is of course the resurrection of Jesus. It would be possible to understand this statement in an utterly trivial and superficial way, simply as a reward for a supremely difficult job finally completed, or perhaps as the sign that, since Jesus was divine, the whole thing had been an elaborate charade. Unfortunately, I suspect that there are some Christians who think in patterns like that. But the resurrection is far, far more than anything of the kind. Evil is the force of anti-creation, anti-life, the force which opposes and seeks to deface and destroy God's good world of space, time and matter, and above all God's image-bearing human creatures. That is why death, as Paul saw so graphically in 1 Corinthians 15:26, is the final great enemy. But if in any sense this evil has been defeated—if it is true, as the Gospel writers have been trying to tell us, that evil at all levels and of all sorts had done its worst and that Jesus throughout his public career and supremely on the cross had dealt with it, taken its full force, exhausted it— why then, of course, death itself had no more power.

"One short sleep past, we wake eternally; and Death shall be no more; Death, thou shalt die." John Donne saw clearly what so many modern readers of the Gospels have missed entirely. Indeed we might even say that the Gospel writers were telling their whole story so as to explain why the resurrection happened, to make it clear that this was not simply an odd, isolated, bizarre miracle but rather the proper and appropriate result of Jesus' entire and successful confrontation with evil. It was like the call of Abraham coming after the judgment on Babel; like the dove and the olive leaf after the forty days' rain. It was God's act of new creation after judgment had fallen on the evil of the old.

But at the same moment as we say "resurrection" and for the same reason (as again Paul saw in 1 Corinthians 15), we must say "forgiveness of sins." The two are in fact the same thing. To be released from sin is to be released from death, and since Jesus died in a representative capacity for Israel, and hence for the whole human race, and hence for the whole cosmos (that is how the chain of representation works), his death under the weight of sin results immediately in release for all those held captive by its guilt and power. This is where all the old hymns come into their own, but now with renewed force and deeper meaning. Forgiveness of sins in turn (just as in Isaiah 54—55) means new creation, since the anti-creation force of sin has been dealt with. And new creation begins with the word of forgiveness heard by the individual sinner, as in the matchless scene between Jesus and Peter by the lake in John 21:15-19.

The story the Gospels are trying to tell is a story in which evil and its deadly power are taken utterly seriously, over against the tendency in many quarters today to cling on to an older liberal idea that there wasn't really very much wrong with the world or with human beings in the first place. With a full-blown theology of the cross such as the Gospel writers offer, there is no need to shrink back from the radical diagnosis, since the remedy is at hand. To be sure, it is humiliating to accept both the diagnosis and the cure. But, as our world demonstrates more and more obviously, when you pretend evil isn't there you merely give it more space to operate; so perhaps it is time to look again at both the diagnosis and the cure which the evangelists offer.

The Gospel writers in fact draw all this together in the sequence of three events, which together both set the scene and give the deepest explanation for what was going on.

First, the temple action. Jesus was embodying and expressing the judgment of Israel's God on the temple as the focal point of the life of the whole people, the people who had refused God's call through the prophets and now were refusing it through the Son. Jesus' action, a clear symbol (like Jeremiah's) of judgment to come, pointed the way forward to the sense that now Israel's God would be known not through the sacrificial system but through the launching of a new covenant in which God's people would learn to love him with heart, mind, soul and strength (see Mark 12:28-34 in its context, where most of the surrounding scenes are about the coming destruction of the temple).

Second, the supper. This was Jesus' own chosen way of expressing and explaining to his followers, then and ever since, what his death was all about. It wasn't a theory, we note, but an action (a warning to all atonement theorists ever since, and perhaps an indication of why the church has never incorporated a specific defining clause about the atonement in its great creeds). Perhaps, after all, atonement is at its deepest level something that *happens*, so that to reduce it to a proposition to which one can give mental assent is a mistake at a deep level (for all that such propositions may be accurate signposts to the reality), something of the same kind of mistake that happens when people imagine they can *solve* the problem of evil. Perhaps, in fact, it *is* the same mistake in a different guise. In any case, at the supper the King shares his life with his friends and, more particularly, solemnly makes them the beneficiaries of his kingdom-bringing death. The Shepherd gathers the sheep together for the last time before going off to do for them what only he can do.

Third, the crucifixion itself. The Evangelists tell, through each of the small stories and minor characters which make this narrative so rich and dense, something of what the event means, much as the minor scenes in a Shakespeare play enable the audience to draw out the full meaning of the central plot. Mary of Bethany anoints Jesus for burial; Simon of Cyrene carries the cross; Barabbas goes free; one brigand curses, the other repents; bystanders mock, soldiers gamble, a centurion stops for a moment in his tracks. Jesus on his cross towers over the whole scene as Israel in person, as YHWH in person, as the point where the evil of the world does all that it can and where the Creator of the world does all that he can. Jesus suffers the full consequences of evil: evil from the political, social, cultural, personal, moral, religious and spiritual angles all rolled into one; evil in the downward spiral hurtling toward the pit of destruction and despair. And he does so precisely as the act of redemption, of taking that downward fall and exhausting it, so that there may be new creation, new covenant, forgiveness, freedom and hope.

The Gospels thus tell the story of Jesus, in particular the story of how he went to his death, *as* the story of how cosmic and global evil, in its supra-personal as well as personal forms, are met by the sovereign, saving love of Israel's God, YHWH, the Creator of the world. This, the Evangelists are saying to us, is what "the kingdom of God" means: neither "going to heaven when you die" nor "a new way of ordering earthly political reality" but something which includes both but goes way beyond them. What the Gospels offer is not a philosophical explanation of evil, what it is or why it's there, nor a set of suggestions for how we might adjust our lifestyles so that evil will mysteriously disappear from the world, but the story of an *event* in which the living God *deals with it*. This raises for us all the echoes of the ancient stories of the exodus from Egypt and the return from exile in Babylon, and it is no surprise that the earliest Christians, both the New Testament writers and others on into the liturgical traditions of the second, third and fourth centuries, reached for imagery from both those events to explain what had happened on the cross. This, they are saying, is how God rescues his people from the evil in which they are trapped; and he does so *through* the suffering of Israel's representative, just as with the martyrs, only much more so. This is what it looks like when YHWH says, as in Exodus 3:7-8, "I have heard the cry of my people, and I have come down to set them free." This is what it looks like when YHWH says, "Behold, my servant." As Isaiah says later (Isaiah 59), it was no messenger, no angel, but his own presence that saved them; in all their affliction he was afflicted. And the result of it all is that the covenant is renewed; sins are forgiven; the long night of sorrow, exile and death is over and the new day has dawned.

The Gospels thus tell the story, centrally and crucially, which stands unique in the world's great literature, the world's religious theories and visions: the story of the Creator God taking responsibility for what has happened to creation, bearing the weight of its problems on his own shoulders. As Sydney Carter put it in one of his finest songs, "It's God they ought to crucify, instead of you and me." Or, as one old evangelistic tract put it, the nations of the world got together to pronounce judgment on God for all the evils in the world, only to realize with a shock that God had already served his sentence.

RESULTS: ATONEMENT AND THE PROBLEM OF EVIL

How then can we put together the question of atonement and the problem of evil?

The first thing to say is that theories of atonement are all, in themselves, *abstractions* from the real events. The events—the flesh-and-blood, time-and-space happenings—are the reality which the theories are trying to understand but cannot replace. In fact, the stories are closer to the events than the theories, since it is through the narratives that we are brought in touch with the events, which are the real thing, the thing that matters. And it is through other events in the present time that we are brought still closer: both the Eucharist, which repeats the meal Jesus gave as his own interpretation of his death, and the actions of healing, love and forgiveness through which Jesus' death becomes a fresh reality within the still broken world.

Having said that, I find myself compelled toward one of the

well-known theories of atonement, of how God deals with evil through the death of Jesus, not as a replacement for the events or the stories nor as a single theory to trump all others, but as a theme which carries me further than the others toward the heart of it all. I refer to the *Christus Victor* theme, the belief that on the cross Jesus has won the victory over the powers of evil. Once that is in place, the other theories come in to play their respective parts. For Paul, Jesus' death clearly involves (for example in Romans 8:3) a *judicial* or *penal* element, being God's proper *No* to sin expressed on Jesus as Messiah, as Israel's and therefore the world's representative. This is the point at which the recognition that the line between good and evil runs right through the middle of me, and of every one of us, is met by the gospel proclamation that the death of Jesus is "for me," in my place and on my behalf. Because as Messiah he is Israel's and the world's representative, he can stand in for all: for our sake, writes Paul, God made him who knew no sin to be sin, to be an offering for sin, on our behalf (2 Corinthians 5:21). Throughout the New Testament, this death is therefore seen as an act of *love*, both the love of Jesus himself (Galatians 2:20) and the love of the God who sent him and whose bodily self-expression he was (John 3:16; 13:1; Romans 5:6–11; 8:31–39; 1 John 4:9–10). Within these, not as the foundation but as the outworking, we see that Jesus' suffering and death are an *example* of how we are summoned to love one another in turn.

In all this, we must remind ourselves that we are speaking and thinking within the realm of *eschatology*, of God's purposes working through history toward a moment of climax. That is to say, what is achieved on the cross is not a timeless, abstract accomplishment located, if anywhere, among Plato's forms, well away from the reality of space-time history. It is not enough to say that God will eventually make a new world in which there will be no more pain and crying; that does scant justice to all the evil that has gone before. We cannot get to the full solution to the problem of evil by mere progress, as though, provided the final generation was happy, the misery of all previous generations could be overlooked or even justified, as in the appalling line in a hymn: "Then shall they know, they that love him, how all their pain is good," a kind of shoulder-shrugging acquiescence in evil which the New Testament certainly does not authorize. No, all theories of atonement adequate to the task must include both a backward look (seeing the guilt, sin and shame of all previous generations heaped up on the cross) and a forward dimension, the promise that what God accomplished on Calvary will be fully and finally implemented. Otherwise the cross becomes merely an empty gesture, ineffective unless anyone happens to notice it and be influenced by it to act in a particular way.

This is where the *personal* meaning of the cross becomes very clear. There will be a time when I—even I, sinner that I am!—will be totally sinless, when God has completed the work of grace within me. But I already enjoy, in anticipation of that future fact, *forgiveness* in the present and *the new life of the Spirit* that is made available precisely when Jesus has been "glorified" by being "lifted up" on the cross (John 7:39; 20:22). And, as we should expect granted the tight sacramental link between Eucharist and cross, the Eucharist embodies and expresses the first of these (forgiveness) and strengthens and enables the second (the life of the Spirit). The personal message of Good Friday, expressed in so many hymns and prayers which draw on the tradition of the Suffering Servant (Isaiah 53) and its New Testament outworking, comes down to this: "See all your sins on Jesus laid"; "The Son of God loved me and gave himself for me"; or, in the words which Jesus spoke at the Supper but which God spoke on Good Friday itself: "This is my body, given for you." When we apply this as individuals to today's and tomorrow's sins, the result is not that we are given license to sin because it's all been dealt with anyway but rather that we are summoned by the most powerful love in the world to live by the pattern of death and resurrection, repentance and forgiveness, in daily Christian living, in sure hope of eventual victory. The "problem of evil" is not simply or purely a "cosmic" thing; it is also a problem *about me*. And God has dealt with that problem on the cross of his Son, the Messiah. That is why some Christian traditions venerate the cross itself, just as we speak of worshiping the ground on which our beloved is walking. The cross is the place where, and the means by which, God loved us to the uttermost.

We shall explore the significance of forgiveness more fully in the final two chapters. But it is time now to return to the larger dimensions of the problem of evil as expounded in the first chapter, and to see the ways in which the cross enables us to approach them in a fresh way.

In chapter one I spoke of the shallow analysis of evil and the immature reactions which it produces. It is fascinating that the best known of the Gospel "atonement" passages occurs, in fact, in the context of a sharp saying of Jesus about the nature of political power and the subversion of it by the gospel events themselves. The request of his disciples James and John that they should sit on either side of Jesus in his kingly power (Mark 10:35-45) is a political question which receives a political answer: earthly rulers lord it over their subjects, but it must not be so among you. Rather, those who are great must be servants, and those who are chief must be slaves of all because the Son of Man came not to be served but to serve and to give his life as a ransom for many.

This evocation of Isaiah 53 (exactly, in fact, as in Isaiah 40—55 as a whole!) sits in the middle of the *political analysis of empire* and subverts it by showing how all the traditions of Israel, the people through whom God would address and solve the problem of the world's evil, come to a point which overturns Babylon and its ways. We find the same point in Luke 9:54, where once more James and John want to do things in the world's way, calling down fire from heaven on their enemies. Jesus' rebuke to them is directly cognate with "Father, forgive them" in Luke 23:34.

What then is the result? The call of the gospel is for the church to *implement* the victory of God in the world *through suffering love*. The cross is not just an example to be followed; it is an achievement to be worked out, put into practice. But it is an example nonetheless, because it is the exemplar—the template, the model—for what God now wants to do by his Spirit in the world, through his people. It is the start of the process of redemption, in which suffering and martyrdom are the paradoxical means by which victory is won. To this I shall return in the last two chapters.

What if, someone will ask, the people who now bear the solution become themselves part of the problem, as happened before? Yes, that is a problem and it must be addressed. The church is never more in danger than when it sees itself simply as the solution-bearer and forgets that every day it too must say, "Lord, have mercy on me, a sinner," and allow that confession to work its way into genuine humility even as it stands boldly before the world and its crazy empires. In particular, it is a problem if and when a "Christian" empire seeks to impose its will dualistically on the world by labeling other parts of the world "evil" while seeing itself as the avenging army of God. That is more or less exactly what Jesus found in the Israel of his day. The cross was and remains a call to a different vocation, a new way of dealing with evil and ultimately a new vision of God.

What, after all, would it look like if the true God came to deal with evil? Would he come in a blaze of glory, in a pillar of cloud and fire, surrounded by legions of angels? Jesus of Nazareth took the total risk of speaking and acting as if the answer to the question were this: when the true God comes back to deal with evil, he will look like a young Jewish prophet journeying to Jerusalem at Passover time, celebrating the kingdom, confronting the corrupt authorities, feasting with his friends, succumbing in prayer and agony to a cruel and unjust fate, taking upon himself the weight of Israel's sin, the world's sin: Evil with a capital E. When we look at Jesus in this way we discover that the cross has become for us the new temple, the place where we go to meet the true God and know him as Savior and Redeemer. The cross becomes the place of pilgrimage, where we stand and gaze at what was done for each one of us. The cross becomes the sign that pagan empire, symbolized in the might and power of sheer brutal force, has been decisively challenged by a different power, the power of love, the power that shall win the day.

The question is then posed to us in the strongest and clearest possible way: Dare we stand in front of the cross and admit that it was all done for us? Dare we take all the meanings of the word *God* and allow them to be recentered upon—redefined by—this man, this moment, this death? Dare we address the consequences of what Jesus himself said, that the rulers of the world behave in one way, but that we must not do it like that? Dare we thus put atonement theology and political theology together, with the deeply personal message on one side and the utterly practical and political message on the other, and turn aside from the way of James and John and embrace the way of Jesus himself? Only so, I believe, can we even begin the task, which I shall address in the two remaining chapters, of working in our own day with mature, Christian and sober intelligence to address the problem of evil which still haunts the world that God loved so much, the world for which the Messiah gave his life.

IMAGINE THERE'S NO EVIL

God's Promise of a World Set Free

I argued in chapter one that despite the beliefs of many over the last century, evil is real and powerful, and that by not recognizing this we have got ourselves into a position where we react to the sudden reappearance of massive evil in an immature and unwise fashion. In the second chapter I examined the classic biblical approach to evil and pointed out that the Old Testament tells the story of Israel as the deeply ambiguous proposal by the Creator God himself to deal with evil, by getting involved in the world he has made, and by more specifically calling a people through whom the problem will be addressed and dealt with. In chapter three I argued that the four canonical Evangelists wrote the story of Jesus and his death in their various ways in order to highlight that event as the climax of the story of Israel, and hence as the point where political and cosmic evil met together and burned themselves out in killing the son of God. Thus, I argued, the Gospels present us not simply with the historical framework for an essentially nonhistorical salvation, but with the story of God's action to deal with evil at every level by letting it do its worst to his own incarnate self. This understanding of the cross is only gained, of course, from the perspective of Easter, at which point the achievement of Jesus in his obedient death begins to be visible, like a great mountain looming up where before those in the valley had seen only a thick, dark cloud.

In the final two chapters I will attempt to sketch out the ways in which this decisive achievement is meant to have its effect. According to the early Christians, what was accomplished in Jesus' death and resurrection is the foundation, the model and the guarantee for God's ultimate purpose, which is to rid the world of evil altogether and to establish his new creation of justice, beauty and peace. And it's clear from the start that this was not intended simply as a distant goal for which one was compelled to wait in passive expectation. God's future had already broken into the present in Jesus, and the church's task consisted not least of *implementing* that achievement and thus *anticipating* that future. I have found in my own work over the last few years that this eschatological framing of the church's task is the most helpful way I know of understanding the challenges, possibilities and limits of what we are supposed to be doing here and now.

In the present chapter, then, I want to explore some particular ways in which this double task of *implementing the achievement of the cross and anticipating God's promised future world* might play out, not so much in our personal lives—that will be the subject of the final chapter—but more particularly in the wider world, where politicians and media have suddenly rediscovered the fact of evil but don't know what to do about it. As I suggested in the last two chapters, we have tended to see what we call "atonement theology" in one box (as having to do with personal salvation from personal sin), and "the problem of evil," including so-called natural evil and the general wickedness of the world, in another box (as constituting a philosophical or logical problem for a good creator, rather than having very much to do with the story the Bible actually tells). I intend by the order of these last two chapters to outflank that problem by painting the larger, global picture first, and only then turning to the much more personal question of how we are to accept God's forgiveness and pass it on to others.

These two chapters, of course, dovetail together. Part of the point of passing on God's forgiveness is that, as South Africa's Desmond Tutu has shown so graphically, this is the most hopeful sign of community restoration and healing known to the human race. We begin, then, with the larger global picture, in order to locate the question of personal reconciliation within that.

One other note about my starting point and method: As the title of this chapter may already have indicated, I intend now to jump, as it were, to the end of the story and work backward from there. Up to this point I have worked forward, tracking the story of the Old Testament and then bringing it to its climax in Jesus and his death and resurrection. That remains the foundation for all Chris-

tian thinking about where we are now and what we should be doing now. But if we simply start from that point and try to grope our
way forward, asking how those foundational events set an agenda
for Christian work in the world, we may find ourselves getting
bogged down. What the New Testament does in two or three key
passages is to point instead to the ultimate future, to the promise
of a world set free from evil altogether, and to invite us to hold that
in our minds and hearts so that we know where we're going. Once
again, we are to *implement* the achievement of Jesus and so to *anticipate* God's eventual world. We have already looked at the
former; it's time to look at the latter.

Imagine there's no evil . . . Unlike John Lennon's famous hymn
to secularism, it's not so "easy if you try"; precisely because of our
muddled thinking about evil itself, we find it hard to imagine a
world from which evil had been removed. I remember one of my
school teachers giving us the assignment to write an essay on what
it would be like if the kingdom of God were to arrive. One of my
friends composed a scornful piece about how nothing much
would happen since people would have no motivation to make
money and get on in the world. How can we think more creatively
about God's promised ultimate future?

It won't do of course simply to imagine a world without terrorists and dictators, without communism and corruption. That
would represent the kind of shallow, dualistic thinking I tried to
expose in chapter one. Nor will it do to reverse the perspective and
imagine a world without capitalism and the exploitation of the
poor by the rich, without B-52 bombers and land mines, without

industrial pollution and half the world crippled by unpayable debt—though there are millions of people in the world who, if invited to imagine a world without evil, would certainly include all of the above on their list of wishes. In each case, there is the danger of dualism, of the us-and-them disjunction which says, " 'Our' way of life is 'good' while 'theirs' is 'bad.' " And this is ultimately not much more help than the ontological dualism which says that the world of space, time and matter is evil and that only the world of pure spirit is good, so that a world without evil would be a world of disembodied spirits sitting on non-spatiotemporal clouds playing nonphysical harps. Imagining that is certainly not easy. Fortunately it is not what we are called upon to do.

In the same way it won't do to imagine that a world without evil is simply a world that has become gradually better and better through a natural process. Imagining a world without evil is not simply imagining what things would be like if we could only work a bit harder and arrive at the utopia that we all know is just around the corner. As I argued before, it's remarkable that this myth of progress has persisted and still persists, despite all the terrible things that have happened in the last century.

But perhaps the important thing is to realize the way in which these false perceptions—the dualist account and the progressivist account—have played out in terms of the way people in our world actually behave and order their lives. If you're a dualist, then there's nothing much we can do to change the world at the moment. Things are going to continue much as they are in this wicked, dark vale of tears until the Lord returns. So we shouldn't even try to make things better; at best, we'd only be repairing a car which is in any case soon going to plunge over a precipice. This is like extreme Marxists arguing against improving the lot of the workers because that would simply delay the revolution.

Dualism of this sort breeds paranoia, the sort that bishops run into a good deal: the system is rotten, and there's a great conspiracy in Congress, in the news media, in Hollywood, in secret movements such as Freemasonry and so on and so on. Conspiracy theory has even got a foothold in the church: we can fight and kick and scream if we want, but there are too many dark plots going on, and what we need is a final showdown between God and evil. This easily plays into a certain view of the demonic, to which we shall turn in due course.

The progressivist, though, takes a very different view. Things are getting better, but the means by which they're getting better is through various kinds of evolution. World War I was justified on this principle: if what matters is the survival of the fittest, then what we need is a good war to sort out who is best fitted to survive. The ethnic cleansing of Native American tribes was routinely justified on similar lines at around the same time. And this in turn gives rise to a new kind of legitimation of empire. If the world is advancing and if somehow God is at work through this advancing world, then the new empires which emerge must be the result of God's work; so why don't you get on board and support what God is obviously doing? That was the argument that convinced a great many Germans to join the *Deutsche Christen* party, the so-called German Christians, in the 1930s; God, so people said, had raised up the German nation to be the new world power. It was against this that thinkers like Karl Barth, Dietrich Bonhoeffer and Ernst Käsemann were reacting.

Today we find a similar argument being advanced to legitimate the new kind of global empire, that of unfettered capitalist growth and the massive global debt that it has produced. The "manifest destiny" of the so-called free world to act in freedom with regard to the rest of the world is a doctrine widely believed and even preached from pulpits in many parts of the United States (I heard it eloquently articulated in Washington's National Cathedral in September 2002). This has led all too easily to wars and rumors of wars.

I want to suggest in this chapter that the Christian vision of world history offers a different way of addressing the problem of evil on the basis of the death and resurrection of Jesus. If we are to implement his achievement, while anticipating the world in which evil has been done away with, we must adopt an approach which is neither that of the dualist nor that of the progressivist. But before we can get to that I must say a few words about the powers of evil, the hidden forces that many theologians have detected behind and within the structures of our world. This is a difficult topic, not to be lightly ventured upon, and yet I must try to summarize in a few words what should really be spelled out at more length.

INTERLUDE: NAMING THE POWERS

Evil has a hidden dimension; there is more to it than meets the eye.

This extra element, I believe, includes a force or forces which are no less real for being difficult to describe. This is, after all, an increasingly common feature of contemporary physics; if scientists had suggested the existence of "black holes" in the universe a hundred years ago they would have been accused of talking nonsense, but we have now accepted that this is the only way to account for the data. Why should something similar be ruled out in other areas of discourse?

In the Old Testament (to recapitulate and develop points that we have made at various stages already) we meet from time to time a figure called "the satan," in Hebrew *Ha Satan.* The word means "the accuser," and in the opening chapters of Job this figure appears as a kind of junior minister in God's heavenly court. He is, as it were, the director of public prosecutions, whose job it is to sniff out offenders and bring them to trial. He asks permission to put Job into a position where he is almost bound to offend. Job does many things in the book, but he doesn't offend in the way the satan was hoping for, namely, by cursing God. Significantly, at the end of the book, though various other people have spoken, the satan is heard from no more. We meet him again in the Chronicler's account of David's census (1 Chronicles 21:1), and as the accusing figure in Zechariah 3:1. We smell his breath not only in the narrative of Genesis 3 but in the apocalyptic visions of Daniel's monsters coming up out of the sea. The satan, it seems, is a nonhuman being, a type of angel, perhaps in some accounts an ex-angel or fallen angel, and he or it (somehow feminists never campaign that the satan should be referred to as "she") comes to be opposed to humankind, and then to Israel, and hence, not surprisingly, to Jesus. The best-known satanic scene in the Bible is surely the temptation story in Matthew 4 and Luke 4, where Jesus recapitulates the testing of Israel in the wilderness, as well as that of Adam and Eve in the garden, this time succeeding where Israel (and humankind) failed.

The satan, it seems, is opposed not only to humankind, to Israel and to Jesus but to creation itself. It is constantly pressing to undo the project of God, the world which God said was very good (Genesis 1:31), when what that world needs—according to the biblical authors—is remaking. The height of the satan's aim, in other words, is death: the death of humans and the death of creation itself. The means that the satan has chosen to bring the world and humans to death is sin; and sin is the rebellion of humankind against the vocation to reflect God's image into the world, the refusal to worship God the Creator, and the replacement of that worship and that vocation with the worship of elements of the created order, and the loss of image-bearing humanness which inevitably results. Death is not an arbitrary punishment for sin; it is its necessary consequence, since the turning away from the living God which constitutes idolatry is the spiritual equivalent of a diver cutting off his own breathing tube. The biblical picture of the satan is thus of a nonhuman and nondivine quasi-personal force which seems bent on attacking and destroying creation in general and humankind in particular, and above all on thwarting God's project of remaking the world and human beings in and through Jesus Christ and the Holy Spirit.

When C. S. Lewis wrote his famous *Screwtape Letters*, he suggested that there were two equal and opposite errors into which people could fall when they thought about the devil. On the one hand, they might take him or it too seriously, imagining the satan as a being equal and opposite to God or to Jesus, and to see direct satanic influence and activity behind every problem and all suffering and misfortune. That danger is still with us. Some today see much pastoral work, and indeed much practical work for the healing of nations and societies, more or less in terms of exorcism. Now I am quite sure there is a place for exorcism. Most pastors are at least aware of situations where it is appropriate. But I am equally sure that Lewis was right to warn against an excessive, morbid interest in the workings of the demonic, an expectation that one will encounter demons behind every tree in the garden.

The opposite error that Lewis imagined was that people might sneer at or mock the very idea of the demonic. Suggest to their minds a figure in red tights, with horns and hooves and a tail, and in sniggering at that they will think they have dismissed, or even disproved, the very existence of the devil. That, I suspect, is behind the downplaying of references to the devil in some of our modern liturgies. Many theologians of the last century have been simply embarrassed by talk of the demonic—until, that is, some political theologians who were too left-wing to be ignored began to use that language to speak of the problems they were addressing (more of that later).

I want to suggest that there is a further error into which people can fall when thinking about "the satan." There is a danger that we

suppose all such language to be merely the projection onto a ficti-
tious, maybe "mythological," screen of those aspects of our own
personalities, our own psyches, that we are uncomfortable with or
want to pretend don't exist. Some of those who cherish the insights of Carl Jung have tried to urge that we should learn to be-
friend our "shadow side" and see what we presently call "evil," or
what we presently shun as satanic, as simply another aspect—perhaps a very creative and hence threatening one—of our full-orbed
personality. That has an attractive and holistic ring to it, and there
may well be truth in the proposal that at least some language about
the demonic is simply a projection of that kind. But both the Bible
and massive Christian experience (to look no further; we could
find plenty of similar evidence in Judaism) over the centuries suggest otherwise.

Each of these false impressions has a grain of truth.

The satan, as portrayed in Scripture and as experienced and
taught about by many spiritual guides, is flatly opposed to God,
supremely to God incarnate in the crucified and risen Jesus Christ.
The claim made by the satan in Luke 4:6—that to him/it has been
given dominion over the kingdoms of the world—is directly challenged by the claim of Jesus in Matthew 28:18: to *Jesus* has now
been given all authority in heaven and earth.

And yet it is wrong to think of the satan as "personal" in the
same way that God or Jesus is "personal"—which is not to say that
the satan is a vague or nebulous force. Quite the reverse: I prefer
to use the term "subpersonal" or "quasi-personal" as a way of refusing to accord the satan the full dignity of personhood while rec-

ognizing that the concentration of activity (its subtle schemes and devices) can and does strike us as very much like that which we associate with personhood. There are undoubtedly foolish and unhelpful ways of portraying the satan, not least in the popular imagination, and we are right to avoid them. But we shouldn't think that by doing so we have eliminated the reality to which these trivializing images point.

Finally, the idea of projection does help us to understand something about what evil is. When we humans commit idolatry— worshiping that which is not God as if it were—we thereby give to other creatures and beings in the cosmos a power, a prestige, an authority over us which *we*, under God, were supposed to have over *them*. When you worship an idol, whatever it is, you abdicate something of your own proper human authority over the world and give it instead to that thing, whatever it is. You call into being a negative force, an anti-God force which is opposed to creation because, being itself part of the transient world, it is bound to decay and die and will, if we're not careful, drag us down with it. This is why I think there is at least a grain of truth in the theory, made famous by Walter Wink, that the inner or hidden forces latent within organizations, companies, societies, legislative bodies and even churches are the sum total of the spiritual energies which humans have put into them, abdicating their own responsibility and allowing the organization, whatever it is, to have it instead. I believe there is more to it than that, but not less.

We see this, I think, in the otherwise puzzling passages in 1 Corinthians 8—10, where Paul is discussing food offered to idols. He insists in chapter 8 that idols don't really have any existence, since there is no God but one. So, you might think, it really doesn't matter whether you go into a pagan temple or not; there is quite literally nothing to it. Not at all, says Paul two chapters later. When pagans offer sacrifice, they do so to demons; and Paul doesn't want you to share in the demonic festivals. "Well," we say to Paul, "are they nothing, or are they demons?" I think Paul really wants to say, "Both."

But they are so in different senses. This goes with the account of evil offered by many great theologians, such as Thomas Aquinas: evil is really the absence or deprivation of good, and yet this doesn't mean it's in any way nebulous or vague or not to be worried about. If there is a hole in the road where I expected solid stone, the fact that there is "nothing there" is very dangerous whether I'm walking, cycling or driving a car. The fact that a rung is missing halfway down the ladder into the basement is neither nebulous nor vague when I'm feeling my way in the dark. And I think the point to be made, whether by Paul or Aquinas, is that idolatry—and sin in all its forms—causes potholes in the road, causes rungs to drop out of ladders, where we and others need them to be. Evil is then the moral and spiritual equivalent of a black hole.

All this is no doubt mysterious, but it is necessary to factor it all into our thinking, even if only (to continue with physics for a moment) in a Heisenbergian sense. Heisenberg articulated the uncertainty principle: when I observe something, the fact that I'm observing it alters the thing I'm looking at, so I can never be sure that

I have grasped it completely correctly. In the same way, there will be an uncertainty factor, a *je ne sais quoi*, in all our moral and spiritual equations, so that however well we organize, however much we pray, however sound our theology and however energetically we go to work, there will be negative forces, perhaps we should say a Negative Force, working against us and for which we must allow.

The good news, according to the whole New Testament, is that this negative force—this quasi-personal, shadowy being or beings—has been defeated on the cross of Jesus Christ. This is part of the full exploration and outworking of what I was talking about in the previous chapter. As I said there, I am inclined to see the theme of *Christus Victor*, the victory of Jesus Christ over all the powers of evil and darkness, as the central theme in atonement theology, around which all the other varied meanings of the cross find their particular niche.

That victory of Christ, and the promise of the final overthrow of evil, thus forms the final element of preparation for the main subject of this chapter. How, granted all this, do we imagine God's new world, the world in which there is no evil at all? How do we then live appropriately between the past victory of Christ over evil and the future world in which that victory will be completed?

WORLD WITHOUT EVIL

The trouble with imagining the future world is that we've all been given the wrong impression. As I have said elsewhere, we shouldn't imagine "heaven" as popularly conceived, but "the new heavens and new earth" of which both Isaiah and Revelation speak. The Bible doesn't give us a picture of the ultimate future as a world of disembodied spirits or cherubs on clouds or a Platonic "Isles of the Blessed" where the righteous get to talk philosophy all day. It's all much more solid, much more real, than that. Revelation 21—22, for all its language full of symbol and imagery, clearly envisages that the reality to which these symbols and images point will be a new creation, an actual world which will resemble our world of space, time and matter in all sorts of ways, even as it will be far more glorious, full of new possibilities, new healing, new growth and new beauty.

Sticking with those last two chapters of Revelation for the moment, we find that we are invited to imagine a *community*, a great multitude of people constituting a city, the city which is the new Jerusalem, the Bride of the Lamb. This is a community from which every type of subhumanity, every sort of diminished and dehumanized behavior, has been excluded (Revelation 21:8, 27; 22:15; the question of how this squares with the judgment scene at the end of Revelation 20 need not concern us here). This community is a place of dazzling *beauty*, as the jewels and the gold and the perfectly proportioned buildings all indicate. It is a place of *healing*, both in the present (Revelation 21:4) and, in a move full of mystery and promise, in the future (Revelation 22:2, where the leaves on the tree of life, growing by the river which flows out of the city, are "for the healing of the nations"). To imagine a community of beauty and healing is to take a large step toward seeing in our mind's eye the world which God intends to bring about through the death and resurrection of Jesus. This is the world toward which we are to direct our Spirit-given energies.

When we come to the Pauline pictures of the same ultimate reality, we first meet 1 Corinthians 15, where the emphasis is on a future world without death. Death—the corruption and decay of the good creation and of humans who bear God's image—is the ultimate blasphemy, the great intruder, the final satanic weapon, and it will itself be defeated. That is the point of the resurrection, which is the main theme of the chapter. Mere "life after death" in some spiritualized sense is not the point; by itself, it would actually collude with death rather than overcoming it. When we think of a world unreachable by death, we tend in Western culture to think of a nonphysical world. But the truly remarkable thing Paul is talking about here is an incorruptible, unkillable *physical* world. New creation is what matters, a new kind of world with a new kind of physicality, which will not need to decay and die, which will not be subject to the seasons and the apparently (to us) endless sequence of deaths and births within the natural order. God's new world will be the reality toward which all the beauty and power in the present world are mere signposts. But they are true signposts, not (as in Platonic schemes) because they point to abstractions—nonphysical realities—but because they point to a world which will be *more* physical, more solid, more utterly real, a world in which the physical reality will wear its deepest meanings on its face, a world filled with the knowledge of God's glory as the waters cover the sea (Isaiah 11:9; Habakkuk 2:14).

The greatest Pauline picture of the future world is Romans

8:19-25. Creation, writes Paul, has been subjected to futility (Romans 8:20). Don't we know it: the tree reaches its full fruitfulness and then becomes bleak and bare. Summer reaches its height and at once the days start to shorten. Human lives, full of promise and beauty, laughter and love, are cut short by illness and death. Creation as we know it bears witness to God's power and glory (Romans 1:19-20) but also to the present state of futility to which it has been enslaved.

But this slavery, like all slaveries in the Bible, is then given its exodus, its moment of release, when God does for the whole cosmos what he did for Jesus at Easter. This is the vision which is so big, so dazzling, that many even devout readers of Paul have blinked, rubbed their eyes and ignored it, hurrying on to the more "personal" application in the following paragraph. But this is where Paul's whole argument has been going. This is where his great theme of the justice of God—even, we might say, the justification of God, the theme of so many treatments of "the problem of evil"—comes to one of its greatest climaxes. The theme of God's justice has for so long been subsumed in popular readings of Paul under the theme of human salvation that we need to remind ourselves, as a matter of strict exegesis, that the theme stated in Romans 1:16-17 comes to its full expression not simply in Romans 3:21—4:25, not simply in Romans 5:1-11 or Romans 8:1-11, but in Romans 8:19-27. The problem is the same, *mutatis mutandis*, as that addressed in the first-century Jewish book we know as 4 Ezra: unless creation as a whole is put to rights, it might look as though God the Creator had blundered or was weak and incapable, or was actually unjust. No, declares Paul: the renewal of creation, the birth of the new world from the laboring womb of the old, will demonstrate that God is in the right. Romans 8 is the deepest New Testament answer to the "problem of evil," to the question of God's justice. And it is all accomplished according to the pattern of the exodus, of the freeing of the slaves, of the cross and the resurrection, of the powerful new life of the Spirit.

The New Testament invites us, then, to *imagine* a new world as a beautiful, healing community; to envisage it as a world vibrant with life and energy, incorruptible, beyond the reach of death and decay; to hold it in our mind's eye as a world reborn, set free from the slavery of corruption, free to be truly what it was made to be. This is the pole by which we must set our compasses so that we may find our way along the intermediate paths that lie before us. The question of how we can imagine such a world is itself challenging, and I shall return to it presently. But before then, let us explore what it might look like if, with such a picture before us, we begin to anticipate this new world in the present. As Paul insists in Romans 8, all our present life, in anticipation of this future one, is a matter of groaning in the Spirit as we wait for the final gift—even as we are also rejoicing because the victory is already won (Romans 5:1-5; 8:31-39).

THE INTERMEDIATE TASKS

There are five quite disparate ways in which, I suggest, we should be working in the present time to put into practice—on the basis of the victory of Jesus Christ in his death and resurrection—the beginnings, the advance signs of that new world which we are called to imagine. There is no space to do more here than simply name them and indicate in a few sentences the much fuller treatment that each properly deserves.

1. Prayer. In Romans 8 Paul indicates that prayer is a key, central anticipation of the eventual redeemed world order. In that world, redeemed humanity will take its rightful place, worshiping the Creator and set in stewardship over the world, sharing God's sovereign rule (Romans 5:17; Revelation 5:10). The new life of the Spirit, to which Christians are called in the present age, is not a matter of sitting back and enjoying spiritual comforts in a private, relaxed, easygoing spirituality, but consists rather of the unending struggle in the mystery of prayer, the struggle to bring God's wise, healing order into the world now, in implementation of the victory of the cross and anticipation of the final redemption. In prayer we are invited—summoned—to become more truly human, to worship the God in whose image we are made and so to find ourselves interceding for the world he loves. The start of God's address to the world, following the death and resurrection of his Son, is the creation and vocation by the Spirit of a people, drawn from every family, who will live consciously out of tune with the world as it presently is and in tune with the way God intends it to be (Romans 12:1-2: "Do not be conformed to this present age, but be transformed by the renewing of your minds"—a statement that might serve as a title for this chapter), and who, by bearing that tension in themselves and turning it into prayer, become agents of that new world beginning to break into the present one in healing and hope. Prayer thus lies at the heart of the task of God's people, their glorious, strange, puzzling and ennobling vocation.

2. Holiness. The Christian calling to radical holiness of life is likewise a matter of inaugurated eschatology, that is, of beginning to live in the present by the rule of what will be the case in the ultimate future. Christian ethics does not consist of a list of "what we're allowed to do" and "what we're not allowed to do." It consists rather in the summons to live in God's new world, on the basis that idolatry and sin have been defeated at the cross and new creation has begun at Easter—and that the entire new world, based on this achievement, is guaranteed by the power of the Spirit. Romans 8:12-17 thus invites Christians to live as "exodus people," not to dream of going back to the slavery in Egypt but to work hard at putting to death all that is in fact deadly and living the renewed life which the Spirit creates in and for those who are led by that Spirit. Among the clearest statements of this theme is Colossians 3:1-11: "If you are risen with the Messiah, seek the things that are above, where he is," which means in very practical terms that all the things which deface human life here and now—particularly anger and bitterness on the one hand and sexual immorality on the other—must be done away with.

So far we have not strayed much beyond what one might expect as a standard "application" of the message of the cross. Prayer and holiness, for all I have expounded them briefly from an unfamiliar angle (that of inaugurated eschatology), are after all well known as themes of the Christian life. But suppose we were to look more widely; suppose that, if God's justice is after all the main theme of

Romans, we might follow that theme through to questions of justice in the twenty-first century. How might this same approach work its way into some of the issues in our wider world, where the "problem of evil" makes itself particularly felt, where our failure to analyze evil properly and respond to it with mature wisdom has made our world even more of a mess than it was in the first place?

3. Politics and empire. The most obvious place to begin, especially in view of the exposition of Mark 10:35-45 in chapter three, is with the way human governments, authorities and empires behave. If it is true, as Jesus said after his resurrection, that all authority in heaven *and on earth* has been entrusted to him, the Christian view of all human authorities is that they are at most penultimate, not ultimate. They are to be held responsible before the Jesus who died and was raised and who now calls the whole world to account.

This is not to say that human authorities are a bad thing. They are not. God has created a beautiful world, and it was always his intention that human beings should look after it on his behalf. That has not changed with the rebellion of the human race. What has changed, of course, is the capacity of human beings to live up to this calling. God intends human authorities to bring his wise, merciful justice to bear on the world, to keep evil in check. One of the most frightening things about the New Orleans disaster in August 2005 was the breakdown, for a few days, of all law and order; that is chaos come again, where might is the only right and the weak are sitting targets. God hates that kind of situation at any and every level, and calls human authorities to prevent it from happen-

ing. However, because all humans share in the evil which authorities are supposed to be keeping in check, it happens all too easily
that the particular human beings in power at any one time find
subtle or not so subtle ways of using their power to act outside the
law and in their own interests.

In this complex situation, the Christian can never settle com-
fortably for the standard post-Enlightenment right-wing solution
(where strong authorities rule subservient populations) or left-
wing solutions (where revolution and even, ultimately, some kind
of anarchy are seen as the ideal). The Christian (and, for that matter, the Jew, though again that introduces more complexity than
this chapter can handle) is thus under obligation both to honor the
ruling authority, whatever it may be, and to work constantly to remind that authority of its God-given task and to encourage and
help it to perform that primary task: to do justice and love mercy,
to ensure that those who are weak and vulnerable are properly
looked after. One of the great early Christian innovations was taking care of the sick, including those who were themselves neither
Christians nor family members. Medical care, education, work on
behalf of the poor—all these are signs that Jesus is Lord and that
the powers of the world are his servants.

This will, of course, challenge all the vested interests that at the
moment rule the world and speak grandly of "good" and "evil" in
reference simply to those things which serve or, as it may be, op-
pose their own ends. This is as true of those whose financial systems keep whole countries in unpayable debt as it is of those
whose caste systems keep tens of thousands of lower-caste peoples

in squalor and penury. And we should note carefully—as a call to readjust our priorities and our rhetoric as we in the West talk grandly about the rest of the world—that the early Christians, like their Jewish cousins, were not particularly worried about the means by which rulers and authorities came to power. They were far more concerned about what they did once they had obtained power. The idea that once some kind of election has been held the government that results has *carte blanche* legitimacy to do whatever it wants for the next few years is a travesty of the freedom and wisdom which the biblical writers seek and urge.

4. Penal codes. The language of "good" and "evil" is also regularly employed by those who organize systems of criminal justice. Again and again one hears it said or implied that some people are simply "evil" and must therefore be locked up for a long time. Over against this, an older generation of liberal thinkers, alarmed at the thought that there might actually be such a thing as "evil"— which they thought had been banished by act of Congress and better drains—tried to insist that nobody was evil at all, merely misguided, and that the misguiding had been done by society as a whole, so that all of us were equally guilty. The political pendulum has swung between these two extremes: the one side seeking to lock up more and more of the population without realizing that they were thereby creating universities of crime; and the other side trying to look the other way and pretend, with a fine suburban detachment, that everything is really all right after all.

But neither of these embodies the imperative of the gospel. What we urgently need, and what, thank God, is coming to be in some wiser corners of the Western world like New Zealand, is an embracing of *restorative justice*. (I know it is paradoxical to describe the most easterly land mass as part of the Western world, but such paradoxes are characteristic of that wonderful country.) Within such a vision, the whole community is committed to naming evil for what it is and to addressing and dealing with it, not by shutting people away from the embarrassed eyes all around, but by bringing together offender and victim, with their families and friends, to look hard and openly at what has happened and agree on a way forward. That is a hard but healthy model, corresponding to what happens in healthy marriages and healthy individuals. It has about it both the mark of the cross (looking evil in the face and letting its full force be felt) and the hope of a world in which all is known and all is put to rights.

5. International disputes. The same polarization of opinion is clearly visible when things go wrong in international relations, as they always have and, it seems, always will. Once more, these are huge issues and we can only give a summary of what could be expanded at much greater length.

On the one hand, some people claim in effect that might is right. Those who have military and economic muscle have the right to do with it whatever they want. From this point of view, the accidents of human power constitute a divine vocation to go anywhere in the world, to intervene in other countries and to enforce one's will wherever and whenever one wishes. On the other hand, there are many who, when faced with any radical evil in the world, will back off and say that it's only a little local difficulty and that we must allow it to be sorted out locally, if at all: in other words, the politics of appeasement. Each side accuses the other of the obvious excesses to which the different policies lead.

What I believe we urgently need is the extension into the international sphere of that concept of legitimate authority which is underlined in Romans 13, remembering what we said above, that all authority is from God and comes under the universal sovereignty of Jesus Christ. The United Nations and the International Criminal Court are the only bodies we currently have which even approximate to a legitimate international authority. The enormous resistance to both which we have witnessed in recent years, ideologically and practically, and the blatant disregard for international treaties such as the Geneva Convention, are worrying signs that we need good international structures more than ever. There is such a thing as evil, and it is to be addressed and defeated not by ignoring it on the one hand or by blasting away at it with heavy artillery on the other—even with all the smart bombs currently available, still when the shooting starts hundreds of thousands of civilians get killed—but by addressing it with the message and the methods of the cross.

EDUCATING THE IMAGINATION

In order to come anywhere near these goals, we need, as I have said all along, to learn to imagine a world without evil and then to think through the steps by which we might approach that goal, recognizing that we shall never attain it fully during the present age but that we must not, for that reason, acquiesce meekly in the present state of the present world. Once again Romans 12:1-2 comes to mind (see above, p. 119).

But the Christian imagination—shrunken and starved through the long winter of secularism—needs to be awakened, enlivened and pointed in the right direction. Each of these is important. Christians need to sense permission, from God and from one another, to exercise their imaginations in thinking ahead into God's new world and into such fresh forms of worship and service as will model and embody aspects of it. We need to have this imagination energized, fed and nourished, so that it is lively and inventive, not sluggishly going around the small circles of a few ideas learned long ago. And the Christian imagination must be disciplined, focused and directed, as with conscience itself, so that it doesn't simply rush madly about in all directions. It will not do to suppose that any old imaginative world will be as good as any other. The brilliant and explicitly anti-Christian fiction of Philip Pullman is a clear reminder that not all inventive and creative ideas and writings are serving the cause of the kingdom of God.

How can the Christian imagination be reeducated so that we can become conscious of living between the victory achieved by Jesus and the ultimate renewal of all things? At this point we must speak about art. One aspect of being made in God's image is that we ourselves are creators, or at least procreators. The extraordinary ability to bring forth new life—of course through begetting children, but in millions of other ways as well—is central to the mandate the human race is given in Genesis 1—2. To make sense of and to celebrate a beautiful world through the production of ar-

tifacts which are themselves beautiful is part of the call to be stewards of creation, as was Adam's naming of the animals. Genuine art
is thus itself a response to the beauty of creation, which itself is a
pointer to the beauty of God.

But we don't live in the Garden of Eden. Art which attempts to
do so quickly becomes flaccid and trivial. We live in a fallen world,
and any attempt to plug in to some kind of pantheism, worshiping
the creation as if it were itself divine, always runs up against the
problem of evil. At that point, art, like philosophy and politics,
often swings round the other way, and determinedly responds to
ugliness with more ugliness. The British arts world has a rash of
this at the moment: a kind of brutalism that, under the guise of realism, simply expresses futility and boredom. Surely there is a
wonderful opportunity here for Christians with an integrated
worldview and with the longing to love God with heart, mind and
soul, to find the way forward—perhaps to *lead* the way forward—
beyond this sterile impasse.

Once again Paul can help us. In Romans 8 he affirms that the
whole of creation is groaning in travail as it longs for its redemption. Creation is good, but it is not God. It is beautiful, but its
beauty is at present transient. It is in pain, but that pain is taken
into the very heart of God and becomes part of the pain of new
birth. The beauty of creation, to which art responds and tries to
express, imitate and highlight, is not simply beauty which it possesses in itself but the beauty which it possesses in view of what
is promised to it, as an engagement ring is beautiful not least because of the promise it symbolizes, and as a chalice is beautiful

because we know what it is meant to be filled with. If Christian artists can glimpse this truth, there is a way forward to celebrating beauty, to loving God with all the soul, without lapsing into pantheism on the one hand or harsh and negative "realism" on the other. Art at its best not only draws attention to the way things are but to the way things are meant to be, and by God's grace to the way things one day will be, when the earth is filled with the knowledge of God as the waters cover the sea. And when Christian artists go to that task they will be contributing to the integration of heart, mind and soul which we seek, to which we are called. They will be pointing forward to the new world God intends to make, to the world already seen in advance in the resurrection of Jesus, to the world whose charter of freedom was won when he died on the cross. It is by such means as this that we may learn again to imagine a world without evil and to work for that world to become, in whatever measure we can, a reality even in the midst of the present evil age.

CONCLUSION

This chapter has glanced briefly at a wide range of subjects. Each of them could be studied much more fully in its own right. But I hope I have at least indicated the enormous and exciting task which lies before us: that we are called not just to understand the problem of evil and the justice of God, but also to be part of the solution to it. We are called to live between the cross and resurrection on the one hand and the new world on the other, and in believing in the achievements of the cross and resurrection, and in learning how to imagine the new world, we are called to bring the two together in prayer, holiness and action within this wider world. In the next chapter I shall consider more closely how this relates to our learning to live with evil within our own selves and within those around us, as we explore the theme of forgiveness, which has a claim to be at the very center of the Christian gospel. But for now, let us focus on encouraging one another to work toward that new world we are promised, in which the earth shall be filled with the knowledge and glory of God as the waters cover the sea. And let us encourage in particular those who have the God-given gifts to show us that world, to inspire our imaginations, so that we may the more readily and gladly believe in and work for all that God wants us to attempt and accomplish.

5

DELIVER US FROM EVIL

Forgiving Myself, Forgiving Others

When I outlined the problem of evil in chapter one, I argued that it was deeper and more serious than we have usually supposed, both in our culture and in our theology. In the second chapter I laid out a way of looking at the Old Testament in which the story of Israel is presented as being itself the solution, or at least the key to the solution, of the problem of evil, leaving us with a story in search of an ending. Then in chapter three I proposed a reading of the Gospels, in particular the story of Jesus' death, which locates what we have traditionally thought of as "atonement theology" on a wider canvas—namely, the ultimate confrontation between God's plan to rescue the world from evil on the one hand, and on the other hand the forces of evil themselves, both the evil regimes of Caesar, Herod and the Sadducees, and the dark, accusing powers that stand behind them. In the fourth chapter I offered a way of looking at the future and imagining a world without evil in order to see how we might conceive the Christian task in the present not in terms of waiting passively for that future to arrive but in terms of anticipating such a future world in prayer, holiness and justice in the present. This brings us now, in this fifth and final chapter, to the question which lies at the center of it all. "Deliver us from evil," we pray again and again in the Lord's Prayer. How will this deliverance happen—not only to us as individuals (the place where the "problem of evil" really bites is that it's *my* problem and yours, not just a big, floppy cosmic thing) but to God's world as a whole?

The way I have chosen to get to the heart of this question is to reflect on the nature of forgiveness. I am aware of three books in particular which have helped me as I have thought about this topic, and I commend them to anyone who wants to take the subject seriously. The first is one of the finest works of Christian theology written in the last decade: Miroslav Volf 's *Exclusion and Embrace,* which won the prestigious Grawemeyer Award in 2002. Volf, who now teaches at Yale Divinity School, found himself some years ago faced with the question of how he, as a Croatian Baptist, could love his Serbian Orthodox neighbor after all the terrible things the Serbs had done to his country. He realized, not least because Jürgen Moltmann rubbed his nose in it, that if he couldn't answer that question the whole authenticity of his theology was called into question. Those of us who haven't had to live with that sort of issue close-up ought to stand in awe as we watch Volf's powerful Christian intellect wrestling with such a hugely emotive and personally involving question, and facing in the process some of the great cultural and philosophical—as well as theological—issues of our time.

Volf's basic argument is this: Whether we are dealing with international relations or one-on-one personal relations, evil must be named and confronted. There must be no sliding around it, no attempt (whether for the sake of an easy life or in search of a quick fix) to pretend it wasn't so bad after all. Only when that has been done, when both evil and the evildoer have been identified as what and who they are—this is what Volf means by "exclusion"—can there be the second move toward "embrace": the embrace of the one who has deeply hurt and wounded us or me. Of course, even then this may not happen if the perpetrator of the evil refuses to see his or her action in that light. But if I have named the evil and done my best to offer genuine forgiveness and reconciliation, I am free to love the person even if they don't want to respond. This brief summary has scarcely done justice to Volf's massive argument, which is both intellectually towering and deeply challenging at a personal and corporate level.

The second book, by the dean of Duke Divinity School, L. Gregory Jones, is called *Embodying Forgiveness*. Jones delves into the pastoral and personal details of what forgiveness actually is and how, as Christians, we can live it out. It is surprising, granted the central place this message has in the New Testament and the teaching of Jesus himself, how little teaching seems to be given on this subject in the church as a whole. There is a wealth of pastoral and theological wisdom in this book from which every Christian community as well as every individual could learn a great deal.

The third book is much more overtly practical and indeed political, though the theological foundations are rock solid underneath. I refer to Desmond Tutu's breathtaking *No Future Without Forgiveness*. The world knows—though sometimes it likes to pretend it doesn't—what Tutu has achieved in South Africa through the Commission for Truth and Reconciliation. I have no hesitation in saying that the fact of such a body even existing, let alone doing the work it has done, is the most extraordinary sign of the power of the Christian gospel in the world in my lifetime. We only have to think for a moment of how unthinkable such a thing would have been twenty-five years ago, or indeed how unthinkable such a thing would still be in Beirut, Belfast or (God help us) Jerusalem to see that something truly remarkable has taken place for which we should thank God in fear and trembling. Though most Western journalists have taken little notice of it, the fact of white security forces and black guerillas both confessing in public to their violent and horrific crimes is itself an awesome phenomenon. And with those confessions, the families of the tortured and murdered have been able for the first time to begin the process of true grieving, and thereby at least to contemplate the possibility of being able to forgive, and so to pick up the threads of their lives instead of being themselves overwhelmed with continuing anger and hatred. This whole project signals a way of being human which is different from the sub-Christian versions on offer in much of the Western world. It thereby acts as a signpost toward the answer to the problem of evil itself, or at least such an "answer" as is open to us in the present age.

Reflect for a moment on the inner dynamic of forgiveness. Many readers will be familiar with the point, perhaps through knowing something about pastoral psychology, but fewer will have connected it with the larger overall problem of evil itself. The fact is that when we forgive someone we not only release *them* from the burden of our anger and its possible consequences; we release *ourselves* from the burden of whatever it was they had done to us, and from the crippled emotional state in which we shall go on living if we don't forgive them and instead cling to our anger and bitterness. Forgiveness, then—including God's forgiveness of us, our forgiveness of one another and our forgiveness even of ourselves—is a central part of deliverance from evil. What I want to do in this chapter is first to explore this point in relation to the larger problem of evil itself (that is, in relation to God and the world and the ultimate resolution of all things), and then to explore what it might mean for us to anticipate this final resolution in our own personal and communal lives.

GOD'S FINAL VICTORY OVER EVIL

I shall begin by looking at the ultimate victory of God over evil. I have ruled out in previous chapters any possibility that the problem of evil can be solved in terms of a developmental progress or evolution. If the world gradually gets better and better until it turns into a utopia—though we should in any case be appropriately cynical about such a possibility—that would still not solve the problem of all the evil that has happened up to that point. I have also ruled out, to the disappointment (I fear) of some, any immediate prospect of finding an answer to the question of where evil came from in the first place and what it's doing in God's good creation. But we can and must address the question: When God eventually makes the new heavens and new earth promised in Revelation 21; when God eventually sets creation free from its bondage to decay to share the freedom of the glory of God's children as promised in Romans 8; when God is eventually "all in all," having defeated all enemies including death itself as proclaimed in 1 Corinthians 15—when all this comes to pass, how is it that in this new world there will not only be no evil but no residual anger or resentment, no burden of guilt still to bear, for all the evil that has happened down the long millennia to that point?

The answer, I suggest, lies in three places, one of which we looked at two chapters ago and the other two of which are the subject of this chapter. First, the death of Jesus himself is seen consistently (albeit multifacetedly) throughout the New Testament as the means whereby evil is confronted and dealt with. It is defeated and its power is exhausted, for all that it appears—as the early Christians were only too aware—to have a continuing virulence even after this heavy defeat. But second, and based likewise on the death of Jesus, God will forgive; and with that forgiveness God will not only release the world from its burden of guilt but will also, so to speak, release himself from the burden of always having to be angry with a world gone wrong. And, third, in the full outworking of the victory of the cross God will win the final victory over the forces of evil, chaos and death, demonstrating them to be intruders into his good world and overthrowing all the power they have arrogated to themselves. I am thus taking Desmond Tutu's title, *No Future Without Forgiveness*, and suggesting that not only is this true for human communities as they try to advance beyond the stalemate of mutual hostility and recrimination; it is also true at a cosmic level, true for God himself. And if this is so it makes it all the more urgent that we learn to live in this way as we seek in the present to anticipate God's promised future.

It is only forgiveness, I suggest, that can make sense of the stunning future prospect held out to us in passages like those I've already mentioned (Revelation, Romans, 1 Corinthians), and picked up in the daring lines so well known both from Julian of Norwich and, echoing her, T. S. Eliot: "All shall be well, and all manner of thing shall be well." Out of context, that statement of hope can become part of the problem rather than a glimpse of the solution; set within an easygoing liberal or progressive optimism, it's a way of shrugging one's shoulders and saying, "Well, it'll all pan out somehow, so we don't need to worry that much." Of course for both Julian and Eliot it couldn't be like that. Julian was extremely down-to-earth and realistic about the actual world and its pains and puzzles; and Eliot only gets to "Little Gidding," with that marvelous refrain, at the end of the *Four Quartets* in which there is so much doubt and death, and indeed toward the end of a career which had seen *Ash Wednesday* and *The Waste Land* among its highlights.

We can glimpse in that long career something of the rhythm of

Miroslav Volf's *Exclusion and Embrace*. Eliot, it seems, first had to renounce the evil he saw all around; only then did he discover how to speak not of optimism but of hope. But we who grew up in the 1960s, 1970s and 1980s learned all too easily to go straight for the "embrace" without bothering about the "exclusion." It can't be done. Volf's book marks the final demolition of the older, soggy, easygoing liberal theology that thought it could say, "All shall be well," without going through the death of fire and water of which Eliot spoke earlier in the poem. The theological question which underlies this dilemma can be simply put: How can it be possible, let alone right, for God to bring about a situation where all is genuinely well, and all manner of thing is truly well, granted all that has happened and, God help us, continues to happen?

This is the problem faced in the majestic throne room scene in Revelation 4—5. The four living creatures are singing "Holy, holy, holy" and the elders are casting their crowns before the throne; but the one who sits on the throne holds a scroll written on the inside and the outside, sealed with seven seals, and nobody can be found worthy to open it and break its seals. The way to God's unfolding purposes to put the world to rights, to complete the whole project of creation, appears to be blocked, since God has made the world in such a way that it must be looked after by human stewards, and no human being is capable of taking God's plan forward. This is Revelation's statement of the problem of evil: God has a plan for the world; but unless he is to unmake creation itself, which is designed to function through the stewardship of God's image-bearing creatures—the human race—it looks as though the plan cannot come to fruition. And this is Revelation's statement of the answer: the Lamb has conquered, has defeated the powers of evil. And now (Revelation 5:9-10) the Lamb has ransomed people from every nation in order to make them a royal priesthood, serving God and *reigning on the earth.*

This theme, so frequent in the New Testament and so widely ignored in Christian theology, is part of the solution to the problem. It isn't that the cross has won the victory, so there's nothing more to be done. Rather, the cross has won the victory as a result of which there are now redeemed human beings getting ready to act as God's wise agents, his stewards, constantly worshiping their Creator and constantly, as a result, being equipped to reflect his image into his creation, to bring his wise and healing order to the world, putting the world to rights under his just and gentle rule. A truly biblical ecclesiology should focus not so much on the fact that the church is the community of the saved but that the church is the community of those who, being redeemed through the cross, are now to be a kingdom and priests to serve God and to reign on the earth. Our fear of triumphalism on the one hand, and on the other hand our flattening out of our final destiny into talk merely of "going to heaven," have combined to rob us of this central biblical theme. But until we put it back where it belongs we won't see how the New Testament ultimately offers a solution to the problem of evil.

God, then, will put the world to rights and will do so in a manner consistent with the design and plan of creation from the beginning. And now it should become apparent that God's action in

Jesus—to redeem a people for himself and to set them in authority over the world—leaves God, so to speak, in the clear. Having defeated evil on the cross, God has put evil in a position where it cannot forever blackmail him.

I first met this theme in C. S. Lewis's remarkable book *The Great Divorce*. He gives his hero George MacDonald a speaking part, and has him explain how it cannot be the case that someone who ultimately rejects the love and mercy of God can hold God's new world to ransom. Our culture has gone even further down the road of moral illiteracy since Lewis's day; the only moral high ground we now recognize is that occupied by the victim, or someone who claims to be a victim. We instinctively feel sorry for someone who's left out of the party, someone who doesn't yet seem persuaded that there's an answer to their problems, someone who has not managed yet to abandon their pride and accept the free forgiveness offered in the gospel. Grand-sounding statements of universalism are offered on this basis: it cannot be right, we are told, for the redeemed to enjoy their heaven as long as one soul is left in hell. Of course, by thus appealing to our sense of feeling sorry for the one left outside the party, we put that person in a position of peculiar power, able to exercise in perpetuity a veto on the triumph of grace.

The old phrase for that is "dog-in-the-manger": someone who isn't enjoying the feast and is determined to prevent anyone else from enjoying it either. The apparent right of evil—evil of all sorts, evil past and present—to stand there in the corporate memory and declare it impossible for God's new world to be perfectly good because this deficit, this outstanding moral debt, has not yet been paid—is overthrown on the one hand by the cross, which has defeated the powers of evil, and on the other hand by God's creation of a new world, which will bring healing rather than obliteration to the old one, under the stewardship of the redeemed. God's offer of forgiveness, consequent upon his defeat of evil on the cross, means that God himself, the wise Creator, is at last vindicated.

This, by the way, is why genuine Christian theology is itself a *redemptive* activity. The effort to understand and articulate the way in which the Creator is gloriously right both to have made the world in the first place and to have redeemed it in just this way is itself part of the stewardly vocation of genuine human existence, bringing God's order into the minds and hearts of others and thereby enabling people both to worship the true God and to serve his continuing purposes.

Thus, just as when we offer genuine forgiveness to someone else we are no longer conditioned by the evil that they have done—even if they refuse to accept this forgiveness and so continue in a state of enmity—so when God offers genuine forgiveness to his sinful creatures he is no longer conditioned by the evil they have done, *even if they refuse to accept his forgiveness.* Otherwise the grouch, the sulker, the prodigal son's older brother, occupies the implicit moral high ground forever. This does not explain, as I said, the origin of evil. But it does, I think, help us to understand how it will be that, when God makes the promised new world, there will be no shadow of past evil to darken the picture.

That's all very well, you say. God may forgive evil done in the past. But the evil was done to the Jews in the Holocaust, to the murdered man and his family, to the rape victim, the family decimated by a drunk driver, the relatives of those killed by a terrorist bomb. What right has God to say that this evil can somehow be wiped away, so that it appears not to exist anymore? Is this not simply another way of belittling evil, making it appear that it isn't really as important as all that? And what right has God to say that he forgives the offender when it is Joe Smith, not God, who has really been hurt?

This is where I have a further proposal to make, which needs to be understood in the light of the very precise meaning of forgiveness for which I am arguing throughout this chapter. Just as in God's new world all his people will have passed beyond death, disease, decay and so forth, so that their new resurrection bodies will be incapable of any such thing, so their moral, thinking, cognitive, affective selves will also be renewed. And in that renewal, they will be enabled fully and finally to forgive all the evil done to them so that they, too, will no longer be affected or infected by it.

This takes, of course, a pretty large leap of the imagination for most of us even in our own relatively uninjured lives; when we imagine some of the morally, physically and emotionally outrageous sufferings of people around the world over the last century, it may seem an impossible dream. Yet it is precisely the outworking of the promise of resurrection itself—which of course appears incredible to those who simply study the world of decay and death and forget the Lord of life who lived among us and died and rose again. Just as physical decay and death will have no power over our resurrection bodies, so the moral decay and dissolution threatened by the persistent presence of evil—the gnawing resentment, the unscratchable itch of jealousy or anger, which are the moral and spiritual equivalents of physical decay and disease—will have no power over our emotional or moral lives in the world to come.

We are in fact called to be people of forgiveness in the present because that is the life we shall be living in the future (more about that in what follows). But the point—and this is really the central point of this book, the ultimate answer to this aspect at least of the problem of evil—is not only that in the new world God himself will be beyond the reach of the moral blackmail of unresolved evil, but that we shall be as well. "Sin will not have dominion over you," wrote Paul in Romans 6:14; this can function as a promise about not only our present moral life but our ultimate future bliss. This is how we shall be delivered from evil, how the Lord's Prayer will finally be answered.

I see something of a pointer in this direction in one of the most powerful and poignant psalms, Psalm 73. The psalmist begins by complaining against the wicked. They are always doing evil and getting away with it. He is envious of them (v. 3); they scoff at God and remain at ease (vv. 10–12); they make the righteous think that there's no point in serving God after all (vv. 13–14). But then he goes into God's sanctuary, into the place where heaven and earth meet, and he sees a different story. Ultimately, the wicked are not only not going to get away with it, since they are in fact in slippery places and facing sudden ruin (vv. 18-19); they are going to be like a dream when you wake up (v. 20). They will be a memory that no longer has any power to make us frightened, embittered, jealous or angry. Thus it will be, says the psalmist in verses 21-22, when we look back from the future life and see our present one. We are still prey in this life to bitterness and anger, to jealousy and malice, and though as Christians we fight a running battle with them, we know that they still dog our footsteps. But from the perspective of God's temple, the place where heaven and earth meet and where the future is disclosed, we see a different reality:

> Nevertheless I am continually with you;
> you hold my right hand.
> You guide me with your counsel,
> and afterwards you will receive me with honor.
> Whom have I in heaven but you?
> And there is nothing on earth that I desire other than you.
> My flesh and my heart may fail,
> but God is the strength of my heart and my portion for ever.
> (Psalm 73:23-26)

No doubt there is much more to be said than this, but it is at least a start. The biblical picture of God's new world—a world without sin, injustice, death or any such thing—is not like the utopian dreams of those who think that by sheer progress the world will gradually become a better place, those who build their golden future on the bones of those who have suffered in the past. That is a gross parody of the biblical picture. The New Testament promises a world in which forgiveness will be offered not only by God but also by all God's people. Part of the joy of the redeemed is that, through being able fully and finally to forgive all that was done against them, the redeemed will live and experience a bliss that will recall no shadows of the past, with all its suffering and injustice.

This picture is cognate with another well-known biblical image—an image used by Jesus in the Farewell Discourses about the contrast between the present and the future:

> When a woman is in labor, she has pain because her hour has come.
>
> But when her child is born she no longer remembers the anguish for joy that a human being is born into the world.
>
> So you now have sorrow; but I shall see you again, and your hearts shall rejoice, and no one will take your joy from you. (John 16:21-22)

Part of that joy, I am suggesting, is that not only physical pain but also the mental pain of unresolved anger and bitterness will be done away with, as we are enabled fully and finally to forgive as we have been forgiven.

I am very well aware that all this could leave me wide open to the charge (regularly made by atheists and agnostics and indeed by many Christians) that I am saying the present world doesn't matter so much because everything will be all right in the future one. I have argued against this in various places and have shown that the promise of God's new world and of bodily resurrection is precisely a reaffirmation of the goodness of this present world, not a summons to leave it out of consideration, and that where resurrection is truly affirmed it leads not to a lack of concern with the present world but rather to a determination that the life of the future world should begin to infect the present one as much and as far as possible. My present proposal in fact works in the same way. So far from saying, "Oh well, that's all right then," and leading to a diminution of our present proper concern with evil in all its forms, this vision of God's ultimate future should lead us to redouble our efforts to discover the meaning of forgiveness, and the defeat of evil which it involves, here in the present as well. This brings us to the second half of this chapter.

FORGIVENESS IN THE PRESENT

I have argued so far, no doubt in a somewhat compressed fashion, that the ultimate answer to the problem of evil is to be found in God's creation of a new world, new heavens and new earth, with redeemed, renewed human beings ruling over it and bringing to it God's wise, healing order. I have argued that the continuing presence and power of evil in the present world cannot blackmail the new world and veto its creation because the power of forgiveness, organically linked to the power of Jesus' resurrection, is precisely that it enables both God and God's people to avoid the imposition of other people's evil.

This does not require that all human beings will come to repent and share the joy of God's new world, wonderful though that would be. Indeed throughout the New Testament we are constantly warned that the choices we make in this life, especially the choices about what sort of a person we might become, are real and have lasting consequences which God himself will honor. But we do not have the choice to sulk in such a way as to prevent God's party going ahead without us. We have the right, like the older brother, to sit it out; God has the right to come and reason with us; but the fatted calf is going to be eaten whether we join in or not. Those who accept God's invitation to God's party on God's terms will indeed celebrate the feast of deliverance from evil.

I now want to suggest that part of the Christian task in the present is to anticipate this eschatology, to borrow from God's future in order to change the way things are in the present, to enjoy the taste of our eventual deliverance from evil by learning how to loose the bonds of evil in the present. Jesus taught us to pray, as one of the most extraordinary clauses in his special prayer, "Forgive us our trespasses, as we forgive those who trespass against us." In one terrifying parable Jesus warned that unless we forgive we shall not be forgiven: in Matthew 18, the servant who was forgiven a massive debt but who then refused to forgive a tiny one to a fellow servant had the initial forgiveness revoked. This, of course, sounds harsh, and I shall come back to it presently. But first, some initial remarks to ward off a further charge regularly leveled against the proposal of forgiveness. I am here once more in line with Miroslav Volf in *Exclusion and Embrace*.

The point springs out at us if we think of the meaning of "forgiveness" in three contemporary contexts. Many of us have campaigned for years for the forgiveness of the massive and unpayable debt in the poorer parts of the world. One of the answers we regularly receive from politicians, bankers and others is that you can't simply forgive debts. The world as they know it would come to a stop. People have to learn that they have to pay back what they borrow. Well, yes and no; but in terms of secular humanism or even sheer self-interest, forgiveness of debts often makes good sense, as the debtors are thereupon free to enter into a more mature and cooperative relationship with the rest of the world. The bankers' point is basically that forgiveness undermines the seriousness of debt.

You see the same thing if you tell people in Northern Ireland or in the Middle East that the way forward for them as a community is to forgive. Howls of protest follow any such proposal. When, famously, one man in Northern Ireland declared that he forgave those whose bomb had killed his daughter, many people, including many Christians, accused him of having gone crazy. In the Middle East both the main protagonists embrace religions where forgiveness has never been seen as a duty, let alone as a virtue, but rather as a kind of moral weakness—and by "moral weakness" I don't just mean a failure to keep a moral law but a deficiency in the implicit moral code itself. Nietzsche would have agreed: forgiveness is for wimps. The main moral standard for the main participants in the Middle East conflict is justice. People should be paid back for wrongdoing. To forgive people, they will say, means going soft on justice, by which they mean the full recompense and punishment which both sides believe they are owed because of atrocities committed by the other. It's not just that they don't want to forgive or that they find it difficult. They believe passionately that it would be immoral, totally wrong. It would belittle the evil that has been done. This is, however, no argument against the proposal of Volf and others, for whom a recognition of the evil that has been done is the first stage towards forgiveness, not an alternative to it.

We find the same kind of standoff in debates about that perennially thorny topic: criminal justice. As we saw earlier, the public mood on this subject has swung this way and that over the last few decades. Criminals are evil and should be locked up (or worse). Criminals are victims of "the system" and should be pitied. Criminals are sick and should be cured. Then back to the beginning: victims of crime are the real victims, and we should care for them and ignore the needs (or rights) of criminals. Some Western countries have experimented with various types of restorative justice, notably those in which (with an idea borrowed from the older wisdom still found in some more "primitive" peoples!) the families and friends of both the offender and the victim are brought together to discuss what has happened and to see what must now be done. But these efforts have not caught on in a big way, doubtless because they do not have a strong appeal for journalists who want a big, easy headline or for politicians who want to give it to them. Few people today would suppose we've found the right way forward.

This is in fact one of the many sharp edges of "the problem of evil." Evil isn't simply a philosophers' puzzle but a reality which stalks our streets and damages people's lives, homes and property. The quest for a solution is not a quest for an intellectually satisfying answer to the problem of why evil is there in the first place. Rather, the quest for a solution to the problem of evil is a search for ways in which the healing, restorative justice of the Creator God himself—a justice which will one day suffuse the whole creation—can be brought to bear, in advance of that ultimate reality, within the present world of space, time, matter and messy realities in human lives and societies. Faced with that challenge, much of the agonizing over evil as a problem in philosophy or theology is exposed as displacement activity, as moaning over spilled milk instead of mopping it up.

What, then, might be done? Most of us would probably favor some kind of penal code which faced the fact that there are indeed some hardened criminals, some of whom are pathologically incapable of living humanely in the world, who are unlikely ever to be reformed, and who need—for the sake of everyone else as well as because of the need for punishment—to spend most of their lives locked up. Most people who have anything much to do with the reality of prison life in the Western world at least know that we are putting into prison alongside such people a great many others who have drifted into petty crime or trivial technical offenses and who, if other forms of punishment could be found (such as compulsory community service, particularly in areas of great need and poverty), could escape that life, put their past behind them and live as responsible and creative members of society. But whenever we try to do this it seems there are always plenty of people who accuse us of going soft on crime itself, of not taking evil seriously. The argument begins to have a familiar ring. As we saw in the first chapter, we seem condemned to oscillate between those who don't think evil really matters and those who want to lash out wildly whenever they notice it.

These three examples—the global economy, international and interracial tension, and criminal justice—function as litmus tests for the problem of forgiveness, the problem which we all meet at a much more personal and intimate level. When someone has done something hurtful to us, how are we to react? Some will respond at once with the command to forgive; and they have Jesus himself, in his exceptionally stern sayings such as those in Matthew 18, to back them up. But when one person urges this duty of forgiveness upon us, another will immediately say, "But that implies you're letting them get away with it," or "But that means you're not taking evil seriously." This is the problem which Volf highlights and addresses in his book.

The point we desperately need to grasp is that *forgiveness is not the same thing as tolerance*. We are told again and again today that we must be "inclusive"; that Jesus welcomed all kinds of people just as they were; that the church believes in forgiveness and therefore we should remarry divorcees without question, reinstate employees who were sacked for dishonesty, allow convicted pedophiles back into children's work—actually, we don't normally say the last of these, which shows that we have retained at least some vestiges of common sense. But forgiveness is not the same as tolerance. It is not the same as inclusivity. It is not the same as indifference, whether personal or moral. Forgiveness doesn't mean that we don't take evil seriously after all; it means that we do.

In fact it means we take it doubly seriously. To begin with, it means a settled determination to name evil and to shame it; without that there is, after all, nothing to forgive. To follow that, forgiveness means that we are equally determined to do everything in our power to resume an appropriate relationship with the offender after evil has been dealt with. Finally, forgiveness means that we have settled it in our minds that we shall not allow this evil to determine the sort of people we shall then become. That is what forgiveness is all about. It is tough: tough to do, tough to receive— and tough also in the sense that once it's really happened, forgiveness is strong, unlike a soggy tolerance which merely takes the line of least resistance.

Let me develop this point a little further. Forgiveness doesn't mean "I didn't really mind" or "it didn't really matter." I did mind and it did matter, otherwise there wouldn't be anything to *forgive* at all, merely something to adjust my attitudes about. We hear a lot today about people needing to adjust their attitudes to things they formerly thought wrong; but that's not forgiveness. If I have a wrong attitude toward someone, and if I need to adjust my attitude, if anything, it's me who needs forgiveness, for my misguided earlier stance.

Nor is forgiveness the same as saying, "Let's pretend it didn't really happen." This is a little trickier because part of the point of forgiveness is that I am committing myself to work toward the point where I can *behave as if* it hadn't happened. But it did happen, and forgiveness itself isn't pretending that it didn't; forgiveness is looking hard at the fact that it did and making a conscious choice—a decision of the moral will—to set it aside so that it doesn't come as a barrier between us. In other words, forgiveness presupposes that the thing which happened was indeed evil and cannot simply be set aside as irrelevant. Along that route lies suppressed anger and a steady distancing of people who no longer trust one another. A much better plan is to put things out on the table, as indeed the New Testament commands us to do, and deal with them.

All of which brings us to that most challenging of biblical chapters, Matthew 18. Here Jesus takes the Jewish law about bringing charges against a neighbor and develops it to fit the situation among his own followers. We need to put Matthew 18:15-20 on the one hand alongside Matthew 18:21-22 on the other. There are, I suspect, all too many who will do the one and not the other, or the other and not the one.

> If another member of the church sins against you, go and point out the fault when the two of you are alone. If the member listens to you, you have regained that one. But if you are not listened to, take one or two others along with you, so that every word may be confirmed by the evidence of two or three witnesses. If the member refuses to listen to them, tell it to the church; and if the offender refuses to listen even to the church, let such a one be to you as a Gentile and a tax collector. Truly I tell you, whatever you bind on earth will be bound in heaven, and whatever you loose on earth will be loosed in heaven. Again, truly I tell you, if two of you agree on earth about anything you ask, it will be done for you

by my Father in heaven. For where two or three are gathered
in my name, I am there among them. (Matthew 18:15-20)

This passage makes it quite clear what the command to forgive
does *not* mean. It does not mean letting people get away with
things. Here again is Volf's "exclusion." If someone has done something wrong even at a personal level, the right thing to do is not to
gossip about it, not to tell everybody else, not to allow resentment
to build up and fester, and certainly not to begin plotting revenge.
The right thing to do is to go and tell them directly. Unfortunately,
the people who are best at doing this, in my experience, are the
people who actually rather enjoy telling other people that they're
out of line. Perhaps the only real qualification for doing it is if you
know, deep down, that you would much rather not have to do it,
and you have to pray for grace and courage to go and knock on
the door in the first place.

It gets worse. If the person refuses to listen to you, if they won't
face up to the problem, you must take another Christian with you;
and then, if you are still refused, you must tell the assembly of
God's people. This is hugely serious, and I don't think most of us
have even begun to come to grips with it. We would probably have
to, of course, if it were a financial irregularity or perhaps a sexual
scandal at the heart of the life of the local church—though even
there, alas, people sometimes do their best to look the other way
and hope the problem will disappear. Mostly, however, we have
tightened up on such matters these days, even though (sadly) this
has often been forced on us from outside rather than generated
from within. But what Jesus is insisting is that we should keep

short accounts with one another, should live as a family not prepared to go to bed at night if there is something unresolved between us. As Paul advises in Ephesians 4:26, we shouldn't let nightfall find us still angry. That's difficult; but it's deeply, seriously wise and therapeutic, both for ourselves when we feel angry and for those against whom that anger may be directed.

But the hard, high demand of looking one another in the eye and speaking the truth even when we know it will hurt is balanced at once by the equally hard, high demand of constant forgiveness. Notice the symbolic depth of what Jesus is asking for. "Shall I forgive my brother seven times?" asks Peter. "No," says Jesus, "not seven times, but seventy times seven." For any first-century Jew who knew the scriptures, the echo would be clear. Daniel asks the angel how long the exile in Babylon will go on. Will it be seventy years, as Jeremiah had foretold? No, says the angel, not seventy years, but seventy times seven (Daniel 9:2, 24). This is how long it will take—note this—"to finish the transgression, to put an end to sin, and to atone for iniquity; to bring in everlasting righteousness." The exile in Babylon was the result of Israel's sin; God has to deal not only with the exiled state of his people but with the root causes in their own wickedness. What Jesus is saying is that the new age is here, the age of forgiveness, and that his people are to embody it.

Behind this again lies the Jubilee commandment in Leviticus: when seven is multiplied by seven, debts must be forgiven. It is not clear just how thoroughly this was kept at any period in ancient Israel, but it forms a clear—and to us deeply countercultural—boundary marker within the divinely ordered social and economic life of God's people. It is one of those commands which the church has cheerfully ignored for long years and is only now rediscovering, in the light of the massive economic inequity of today's world.

All this stands behind the command to pray, in the Lord's Prayer, "Forgive us our trespasses, as we forgive those who trespass against us." Jesus is declaring, with every breath he takes, that the new covenant is being inaugurated in his own work, and that his followers are to live as returned-from-exile people, and hence as forgiveness-of-sins people. The command to forgive is not simply a new and tougher piece of ethics for high flying moralists to attempt. It follows directly from the situation Jesus has inaugurated in his own work and would seal in his death and resurrection. "This cup," he said, "is the new covenant in my blood, shed for you and for many for the forgiveness of sins." The atonement is not simply an abstract transaction making God's forgiveness available to those who want it. It was and is the stunning, towering achievement by which evil itself was defeated so that God's new age could begin. And we who claim to follow Jesus can make that claim good only insofar as we live by the rule of forgiveness— serious forgiveness, not the cheap imitations discussed above. Only so can we live out the proper Christian answer to the problem of evil, which is not a theory but a life, a life which will be vindicated or validated in the age to come when evil is finally abolished altogether.

All this enables us to approach the very difficult parable at the end of Matthew 18 with some hope of success.

"So you see," Jesus went on, "the kingdom of heaven is like a royal personage who wanted to settle up accounts with his servants. As he was beginning to sort it all out, one man was brought before him who owed ten thousand talents. He had no means of paying it back, so the master ordered him to be sold, with his wife and children and everything he possessed, and payment to be made.

"So the servant fell down and prostrated himself before the master. 'Have mercy on me,' he said, 'and I'll pay you everything!'

"The master was very sorry for the servant, and let him off. He forgave him the loan.

"But that servant went out and found one of his fellow servants, who owed him a hundred dinars. He seized him and began to throttle him. 'Pay me back what you owe me!' he said.

"The colleague fell down and begged him, 'Have mercy on me, and I'll pay you!'

"But he refused, and went and threw him into prison until he could pay the debt.

"So when his fellow servants saw what had happened, they were very upset. They went and informed their master about the whole affair. Then his master summoned him.

"'You're a scoundrel of a servant!' he said to him. 'I let you off the whole debt, because you begged me to. Shouldn't you have taken pity on your colleague, like I took pity on you?'

"His master was angry, and handed him over to the tortur-
ers, until he had paid the whole debt. And that's what my
heavenly father will do to you, unless each of you forgives
your brother or sister from your heart." (Matthew 18:23-35)

I have heard good Christian people say that we should not read
this parable out loud at all, or that if we do we should laugh bit-
terly at the final line, since (they say) it is obviously a later editorial
addition to what Jesus himself "must have" said and meant, and a
pretty vicious and distorting editorial addition at that. Is God really that sort of a God? How can he decide to punish people after
all when he had already forgiven them?

But this objection fails to realize how the inner human logic of
forgiveness actually works. Jesus is not giving a kind of arbitrary,
abstract commandment and then saying that if you fail to meet the
test God will not forgive you. He isn't setting the moral bar at an
impossible height and then warning that God will be everlastingly
cross if we don't manage to jump it. He is drawing attention to a
fact about the moral universe and human nature. He is telling us,
in effect, that the faculty we have for receiving forgiveness and the
faculty we have for granting forgiveness are one and the same
thing. If we open the one we shall open the other. If we slam the
door on the one, we slam the door on the other. God is not being
arbitrary. If you are the sort of person who will accuse a neighbor
over every small thing and keep him or her under your anger until
each item has been dealt with (perhaps by your gaining revenge),
then you are also the sort of person who will be incapable of opening your heart to receive God's generous forgiveness. Indeed you

will probably not admit that you need it in the first place.

Here we come back to the point I made earlier about forgiveness: it releases not only the person who is being forgiven but the person who is doing the forgiving. We can probably all think of examples of this. When I forgive you for treading on my toe, I release you from any burden of guilt, any sense that I might still be angry with you when we meet tomorrow, or that I will treat you differently in the future or try to get even with you. But I also release myself from having to go to bed cross, from having to toss and turn wondering how to gain my revenge. When we go up the scale from treading on toes to far more serious offenses, forgiveness can mean not only that I release you from the threat of my anger and its consequences, but also that I avoid having the rest of my life consumed with anger, bitterness and resentment. And, to put this more positively, it releases both of us into the freedom to continue a cheerful and mutually respectful relationship.

All that could of course sound merely selfish. You could read it as though all I'm really doing when I forgive you is making my own emotional life a bit more comfortable. But here's the catch: If we try to forgive someone else in order simply to clear our own emotional overdraft, it doesn't work. You only get the personal spin-off *as a* spin-off from the genuine forgiveness you have offered. Otherwise you are simply playing self-centered emotional games, and they will backfire. If you try to love someone simply in order to be loved in return, what you are offering isn't love, and what you get back won't be love either. Sooner or later, if you go down that road, you will be worse off than if you'd never tried it in the first place.

The command to forgive one another, then, is the command to bring into the present what we are promised for the future, namely the fact that in God's new world all shall be well, and all manner of thing shall be well. It will still be possible for people to refuse forgiveness—both to give it and to receive it—but they will no longer have the right or the opportunity thereby to hold God and God's future world to ransom, to make the moral universe rotate around the fulcrum of their own sulk. And, as with all attempts to bring elements of God's future world into the present one, the only way is through the appropriate spiritual disciplines. It doesn't "just happen." None of us does it, as we say, "by nature." We need to learn *how* to do it; and it's all the more difficult because the church has not been teaching us this lesson. This is where we need to understand, better than we usually have, the biblical account of inaugurated eschatology, of living in the present in the light of the future. Understanding this is difficult to begin with, but it gets easier as you try. Living by it likewise requires hard work: prayer, thought, moral attention to your own state of mind and heart, and moral effort to think and behave in certain ways when "what would come naturally" would be something very different.

The tough, many-sided offer of forgiveness should be the ultimate aim as we think about the problems of global empire and international debt, of criminal justice and the problem of punishment, of war and international conflict. In each of these spheres there is a task of naming evil and finding appropriate ways of resisting it, and at the same time working toward remission, reconciliation, restitution and restoration. My hope is that those who are beginning to see the issues in this light should think through them further, and recognize the many ways in which this central and vital element of the Christian gospel cries out to be put into practice not only in our personal lives and church fellowships but also in our public and political lives, at both the national and the global level.

One more point must be made here. How do we apply to our own selves the prayer at the end of the Lord's Prayer: that we should be delivered from evil? I may believe that God has forgiven me through the death of Jesus. I may begin to learn how to forgive my neighbor. But can I forgive myself? That is a very different question.

Jesus (echoing the Old Testament) told us to love our neighbors as we love ourselves. The first thing to note here is that he wasn't basically talking about feelings. As often in Jewish and Christian thought, "love" is first and foremost something you do, not something you feel; the feelings often follow the actions, not (as in some modern thinking) the other way around. "Loving myself," in Jesus' teaching, does not therefore mean what the modern therapeutic movements mean when they speak of "feeling good about myself." That may or may not be involved. What "love" means first and foremost is taking thought for someone, taking care of them, looking ahead in advance for their needs, in the way that you would take careful thought about, and plan wisely for, your own life.

Christian moralists have sometimes drawn attention to the fact that it's easy, when we find we are called to love one another, to push ourselves out of the picture, to imagine that we are no longer important, to develop a negative self-image. They have rightly pointed out that in order to love our neighbor *as* ourselves we need to love ourselves first, so we know what the standard should be! This point is well known and well taken. But the same applies, more subtly perhaps, to the question of forgiveness. Those with any pastoral experience will have met the person who says, "Well, I know God forgives me, but I can't forgive myself." We can understand what they mean. But it is precisely here, I suggest, that the prayer "Deliver us from evil" comes right home into the human heart, imagination and emotions—or, if you like, the soul, which as I have said elsewhere is really a way of speaking about "who I am in the presence of God."

It takes spiritual discipline to forgive others; it takes a different, though related, spiritual discipline to forgive myself, to echo within my own heart the glad and generous offer of forgiveness which God holds out to me and which, if I'm fortunate, my neighbor holds out to me as well. Here, too, my sense of self-worth comes not from examining myself and discovering that I'm not so bad after all but from gazing at God's love and discovering that nothing can stand between it and me. (What we are doing is drawing down from God's ultimate future, in which I will know myself to be completely loved and accepted because of the work of Jesus and the Spirit.) This astonished and grateful acceptance of the free grace and love of God is what some traditions have meant when they have echoed Paul's language about "justification by faith."

This is central to mental, emotional and spiritual health. Part of the discipline of receiving God's forgiveness, of training our forgiveness-receiving faculty to respond to the gospel, is that we open that same inner faculty as wide as it can go and thus learn the secret not only of *accepting* ourselves—that's one thing, recognizing that I am the person I am and learning to be comfortable with that—but also of *forgiving* ourselves, which is quite another thing. Forgiving myself means recognizing that I have indeed done sinful, hurtful and damaging things to other people, to myself and to the God in whose image I'm made, and that because God forgives me I must learn, under his direction, to forgive myself. Of course, as with all the other forgiving we've been thinking about, this does *not* mean pretending it wasn't so bad after all or that it didn't really happen or that it didn't matter that much. It was bad and it did happen and it did matter. But if God has dealt with it and forgiven you (and if you have made amends as best you can with any other people it may have involved), then it is part of living an authentically Christian life that you learn to forgive yourself as well.

Of course, because it's forgiveness we're talking about, not tolerance or indifference, this will once more mean exclusion as well as embrace. It will mean saying *No* to whatever it was in order to say *Yes* to God and his forgiveness. This will almost certainly take prayer and worship and perhaps the assistance of a wise counselor, but it's the way we are called to go, the way to spiritual health. Those who insist on clinging to a sense of guilt all too easily become, alas, those who then pass on that sense of guilt to others as the burden becomes too great to bear. Part of the answer to the prayer "Deliver us from evil" is that we learn to forgive ourselves, both for our own sake and for the sake of those around us.

CONCLUSION

Where has all this taken us with the problem of evil? I have argued that the problem of evil as classically conceived within philosophy is not soluble as it stands, not least because it tends to postulate a god other than the God revealed in Jesus Christ. When we bring the Bible into the equation, not least the Gospel accounts of Jesus, the picture becomes more complicated but also ultimately richer, and the problem becomes relocated.

We are not told—or not in any way that satisfies our puzzled questioning—how and why there is radical evil within God's wonderful, beautiful and essentially good creation. One day I think we shall find out, but I believe we are incapable of understanding it at the moment, in the same way that a baby in the womb would lack the categories to think about the outside world. What we are promised, however, is that God will make a world in which all shall be well, and all manner of thing shall be well, a world in which forgiveness is one of the foundation stones and reconciliation is the cement which holds everything together. And we are given this promise not as a matter of whistling in the dark, not as something to believe even though there is no evidence, but in and through Jesus Christ and his death and resurrection, and in and through the Spirit through whom the achievement of Jesus becomes a reality in our world and in our lives. When we understand forgiveness, flowing from the work of Jesus and the Spirit, as the strange, powerful thing it really is, we begin to realize that God's forgiveness of us, and our forgiveness of others, is the knife that cuts the rope by which sin, anger, fear, recrimination and death are still attached to us. Evil will have nothing to say at the last, because the victory of the cross will be fully implemented.

We return to the point at which we began. In the new heavens and the new earth there will be no more sea, no more chaos, no more monsters coming up from the abyss. And, as with all Christian eschatology, the best news of all is that we don't have to wait for the future to start experiencing our deliverance from evil. We are invited, summoned, bidden to start living this way in the present. I suspect that the problems this poses for us—the immediate problems of forgiving ourselves and our neighbors, and the practical and political problems of working for a world in which people no longer wish to become terrorists, in which people no longer enslave one another with crippling debt, and in which those who live at great risk of the natural elements receive special protection from civil authorities—are the real problems. The philosophical problems often function simply as a smoke screen behind which we try to hide. And I suspect, therefore, that the more we learn the meaning of forgiveness in our own lives, the more we shall glimpse the deep theological truth that all shall be well, and all manner of thing shall be well, and the more we shall be enabled to anticipate that reality even in the midst of our suffering world.

Notes

Chapter 1: Evil Is Still a Four-Letter Word

page 14   the psalmist describes his despair: See further Psalms 24:2; 33:7; 46:2; 65:5, 7; 66:6; 68:22; 74:13; 89:9; 95:5; 98:7; 104:25.

page 18   I am in implicit dialogue: See in particular, e.g., Susan Neiman, *Evil in Modern Thought: An Alternative History of Philosophy* (Princeton, N.J.: Princeton University Press, 2002).

page 38   as Walter Wink has argued: Walter Wink, *Naming the Powers* (Philadelphia: Fortress, 1984); *Unmasking the Powers* (Philadelphia: Fortress, 1986); *Engaging the Powers* (Minneapolis: Fortress, 1992).

Chapter 2: What Can God Do About Evil?

page 61   Wretched and close to death: Psalm 88:15-18. The NRSV translates the final clause, "my companions are in darkness," but with many commentators and translations I prefer the version in the text.

Chapter 3: Evil and the Crucified God

page 75   I have explored all this: N. T. Wright, *Jesus and the Victory of God*, Christian Origins and the Question of God, vol. 2 (Minneapolis: Fortress, 1996).

page 83   notably *The Challenge of Jesus*: N. T. Wright, *The Challenge of Jesus* (Downers Grove, Ill.: InterVarsity Press, 2000).

Chapter 4: Imagine There's No Evil

page 103   Part of the point of passing on God's forgiveness: Desmond Tutu, *No Future Without Forgiveness: A Personal Overview of South Africa's Truth and Reconciliation Commission* (London: Rider, 2000).

Chapter 5: Deliver Us from Evil

page 132   One of the finest works of Christian theology: Miroslav Volf, *Exclusion and Embrace: A Theological Exploration of Identity, Otherness and Reconciliation* (Nashville: Abingdon Press, 1994).

page 133   The second book: L. Gregory Jones, *Embodying Forgiveness: A Theological Analysis* (Grand Rapids: Eerdmans, 1995).

page 157   So you see: N. T. Wright, *Matthew for Everyone,* vol. 2, *Chapters 16—28* (Louisville: Westminster John Knox, 2002).

Subject Index

Abraham, call, 46, 47-48, 49
Addison, Joseph, perception on evil, 19-20
Adorno, Theodor, 31
adultery, 25
akrasia, 36
Al-Qaeda, 24, 27
Amorites, 57
art, and the realization of new creation without evil, 127-28
Ash Wednesday (Eliot), 138
Assyrians, 58
atonement, 156
    Christus Victor, 95, 114
    crucifixion, 92-93
    and eschatology, 95-96
    and evil, 75-76, 77-78, 94-100, 102-3
    in the Gospels, 78-88, 97-98, 131-32
    theology, 78, 79, 88, 103, 131
    see also Jesus
Auschwitz as challenge to the doctrine of progress, 22-23
"axis of evil," 9
Barth, Karl, on the doctrine of progress, 22-23
black holes, 109, 113
Blair, Tony, 9, 16

blame culture, as response to evil, 29
Bonhoeffer, Dietrich, 59, 108
Britain, democracy, 35
Brothers Karamazov (Dostoevsky), 22, 70
Buddhism on evil, 34
Bush, George W., 9, 16
Canaan, conquest, 57
capitalism, legitimation questioned within new creation, 104-5
Carter, Sydney, 94
caste system, 123
censorship, 25
Challenge of Jesus (Wright), 83
chaos, symbolized by the sea, 13-15, 41, 165
Christian ethics, 120
Christianity, response to evil, 40-41
Christus Victor, 95, 114
church
    atonement role, 99-100, 103, 107
    as the community of those who are victorious over evil, 124, forgiveness within, 151, 153-54, 156, 160
Commission for Truth and Reconciliation, 134
community restoration through the atonement, 103

Scripture Index